# Inductive Study Curriculum
## Student Guide

OLD TESTAMENT/*Character Study*

# Joseph

## Surrendering to God's Sovereignty

*Joseph*
INDUCTIVE STUDY CURRICULUM

ISBN 978-1-934884-15-7

1st edition
Printed in the United States of America

# TABLE OF CONTENTS

*Joseph*

Introduction to Inductive Study ............... 5-8

Unit One .................................................... 9-30
### Sibling Rivalry
*Lesson One*     11
*Lesson Two*     15
*Lesson Three*     17
*Lesson Four*     21
*Lesson Five*     23
*Lesson Six*     25

Unit Two .................................................... 31-48
### From the Pit to the Palace
*Lesson One*     33
*Lesson Two*     35
*Lesson Three*     37
*Lesson Four*     39
*Lesson Five*     41

Unit Three .................................................... 49-68
### Feast or Famine
*Lesson One*     51
*Lesson Two*     53
*Lesson Three*     59
*Lesson Four*     61
*Lesson Five*     63
*Lesson Six*     65

Unit Four .................................................... 69-90
### Trust in Tragedy
*Lesson One*     71
*Lesson Two*     73
*Lesson Three*     77
*Lesson Four*     79
*Lesson Five*     83

Appendix .................................................... 91-156
*Observation Worksheets*     93
*At A Glance Chart*     145
*Maps*     147
*My Journal on God*     149
*About Precept Ministries*     155

*Joseph*

1. Inductive Bible Study - _Using the Bible as your primary source_

2. There are _three components_ of Inductive Bible Study:

    a. _Observation_ - _what does the text say_ ?

    b. _Interpretation_ - _what does the text mean_ ?

    c. _Application_ - _How does the meaning apply to my life_ ?

3. Tools of Observation

    a. The _5W and H_ questions

b. Mark <u>key words</u> and <u>people</u>

c. Make <u>lists</u>

4. Tools of Interpretation

a. <u>Context</u>

<u>Context is king</u>! It rules interpretation.

b. <u>Cross-references</u>

c. <u>Word-studies</u>

5. Application

a. _To Know God_ – resulting in _a changed life_

*Joseph*

# Sibling Rivalry

Nearly 4,000 years ago a man named Joseph lived... a man who, like you, faced temptations and trials. You'll meet him first as a young man. His home life may seem familiar. Like many today, Joseph lived in a "blended family" with 11 brothers, only one brother with the same mother. **Strife**, **jealousy**, and **rivalry** dominated his childhood.

Along the way, Joseph fell victim to others' bad choices. But his faith in the One True God and His

sovereign plan provides an epic story of redemption, salvation, and **restoration**. His story can help you navigate the twists and turns in your life. Diligently study and you will learn how to rise above your circumstances and live victoriously... even when your dreams are shattered.

> "They hated him and could not speak to him on friendly terms... When they saw him from a distance and before he came close to them, they plotted against him to put him to death."
>
> - Genesis 37:4, 18

## PRAYER

### ONE ON ONE:

Now as with every study, begin with prayer, asking God to prepare your heart to receive His Word. Pray for diligence and perseverance when life's demands and circumstances compete for your time and attention. Pray that God's Holy Spirit will bless you with knowledge and understanding of His will and ways. Ask God to reveal Himself as you study Joseph's life. At the end of the study, look back at this prayer and record how God answered.

Before you begin the study of Joseph, look at what comes before his story in the book of Genesis. Fill in the puzzle pieces below with the main events and people recorded in Genesis prior to Genesis 37. Briefly describe the event or person in each reference. This establishes the context for Joseph's life.

**Context** rules interpretation! If you don't accurately establish the context (the setting), you can misinterpret the text. If you misunderstand, you won't be able to apply it to your life correctly.

Genesis 1-2

CREATION

Genesis 3

THE FALL

Genesis 4

CAIN & ABEL

Genesis 6-10

NOAH, THE FLOOD

Genesis 11-23

ABRAHAM

Genesis 24-27

Isaac

Genesis 28-36

JACOB & ESAU

Genesis 37

JOSEPH

# LESSON ONE

Although Joseph is mentioned earlier in the book of Genesis, his story begins in chapter 37. You will study and complete your observations on the Genesis 37-50 Observation Worksheets located in the Appendix.

> **Observation Worksheets** *contain the scriptures you will be studying. The text is double spaced and pages have wide margins so you can easily mark words and make notes. They are worksheets for you to complete your observations on!*

1.  Read Genesis 37:1-4.

    a.  Mark references to *Joseph* including pronouns in a distinct color.

    b.  Then look at each reference to see if it answers the 5 Ws and H: who, what, when, where, why and how. These **investigative** questions help you understand what's written.

       Look for:

       • **who** Joseph is
       • **whom** he belongs to or associates with
       • **what** he does
       • **where** he is
       • **what** happens to him and **why**
       • **when** this is occurring
       • **why** he's treated as he is
       • **how** he responds, etc.

    c.  List everything these first four verses tell you about Joseph.

    > vs. 2- 17 years old
    > vs 2- pasturing the flock with his brothers
    > vs 2- brought back a bad report about them to their father
    > vs 4 - loved by Israel more than all his sons because he was the son of his old age
    > vs. 4 Israel made him a varicolored tunic
    > vs 4 Brothers saw that their father loved him more so they hated him and could not speak to him on friendly terms

2.  Now, if you have not completed character studies on Abraham, Isaac, Jacob, and Esau from Genesis, you need to gain a better understanding of Joseph's background.

    a.  Joseph's father is referred to by two names: Jacob and Israel (Genesis 37:1-3). Jacob is the son of Isaac and the grandson of Abraham. God made covenant promises to Abraham, Isaac, and their descendants.

In Genesis 28, He also gave promises to Jacob. Read Genesis 28:13-15 and write down what you learn about God's promises to Jacob.

V.13 God will give land to him and his descendants
V.14 Descendants will be like the dust of the earth
V.14 Descendants will be spread in all directions
V.14 All families on the earth will be blessed in his descendents
V.15 God is with Jacob where ever he goes
V.15 God will bring him back to the land of Canaan; He will not leave him until the promise is fulfilled

b. Genesis 32:22-30 explains how Jacob received his second name, Israel. Write down what you learn about this name: who changed it and why.

- after he wrestled with a man all night
- Jacob's thigh was dislocated and he refused to let go until the man blessed him
- the man changed Jacob's name to Israel "You have strived with God a men and have prevailed."

c. Read Genesis 35:22b-29, and record:

1) How many sons Jacob had.

12

2) Who Jacob's father was and how old he was when he died. Isaac — he died when he was 180

3) Jacob's brother's name.

Esau

4) The birth order of Jacob's (Israel's) sons and their mothers' names are listed in the chart.

Underline Joseph's name and note his mother's name.

---

THE BIRTH ORDER OF JACOB'S SONS

| | |
|---|---|
| Leah | Reuben (born 1921 B.C.) |
| | Simeon |
| | Levi |
| | Judah |
| Bilhah (Rachel's Maid) | Dan |
| | Naphtali |
| Zilpah (Leah's Maid) | Gad |
| | Asher |
| Leah | Issachar |
| | Zebulun |
| Rachel | Joseph (born 1914 B.C.) |
| | Benjamin |

---

3. Now look up the following verses to learn about Joseph's mother Rachel and list your insights.

   a. Genesis 29:16-30

   b. Genesis 29:31–30:8 (This will give you a glimpse of how Jacob fathered so many sons before Joseph was born.)

   c. Genesis 30:17-24

   d. Genesis 35:16-24

4.   What did you observe that helps you understand Jacob's (Israel's) partiality toward Joseph and his brothers' **animosity** toward him?

---

In a time when there are so many blended families as a result of divorce and remarriage, can you see the relevancy of Joseph's story? If you are a child of divorce, Joseph's story will show you that because of the power of God in your life you do not have to be defined by your hurts and circumstances. And if you can't relate to Joseph's family life, you can still learn to be victorious over struggles, temptations, and hurt. And can learn to glorify God in the midst of them.

What gave Joseph the ability to glorify God during his difficult circumstances? Keep studying. If you apply what you learn, you will glorify God just like him.

Today, read Genesis 37, observing and marking to see exactly what the text says.

1. Read Genesis 37:5-11.

   a. List the main characters in this paragraph.

> Whenever you study the Bible, you need to slow down to develop good observation skills. And since the Bible is God's Book, you need to ask God to help you see and understand what He has written and preserved. So always begin your study with prayer.

   b. Briefly summarize the main points of this paragraph.

> When you observe a chapter, begin with the obvious: look for people first. See what the text says about them.

   c. How do Joseph's brothers feel about him? Describe their feelings (from the text).

   d. Mark occurrences of *hated* in Genesis 37:3-11. Draw a dark colored heart with a slash through it ♥. Observe who hates whom, why, and how this hatred came about.

   e. Did you notice another important word repeated several times that helps you understand the text? Write it below then mark it in a distinctive way every time it occurs in Genesis 37:5-11. Also mark pronouns that refer to this key word.

   f. Carefully observe Joseph's dreams and briefly answer the following:

      1) What Joseph dreamed

2) What his brothers understood the dreams to mean

3) What this evoked in Joseph's brothers

4) What Joseph's father understood the dream to mean and what he did with this information

2. In the space below, draw Joseph's two dreams. Don't worry about making them look perfect, just draw them well enough for you to look back at them and remember each dream's main points.

3. Using a 3x5 notecard, create a bookmark of key words and symbols you have used already. Add new key words you discover in the course of the study.

EXAMPLE:

```
┌──────────────────────────────────────┐
│  ┌────────┐                           │
│  │ Joseph │                           │
│  └────────┘                           │
│                                        │
│                                        │
│                                        │
│                                        │
│                                        │
│                                        │
│                                        │
└──────────────────────────────────────┘
```

# LESSON THREE

1. Read Genesis 37:12-17.

   a. Double underline geographical locations in green. (Add "geographical locations" to your key word bookmark.) Trace Joseph's journey on the map located in the Appendix.

   > Pay careful attention to geographical references to answer the investigative question "Where?"

   b. Summarize what occurs in this paragraph in no more than two sentences. Pretend you are telling someone what's covered.

2. Now read Genesis 37:18-24.

   a. Who does "they" refer to in verse 18? When you observe the text, carefully check pronouns to know who they reference.

   b. Do you see key words and synonyms you marked previously in Genesis 37:5-11? If so, mark them the same way. (Hint: Note how Joseph is referred to in verse 19.)

   c. What do Joseph's brothers want to do to him? Look for a key phrase and mark it the same way.

   d. Which brother opposes this idea? Where is he in the birth order? Why do you think he was concerned?

   e. What does this brother suggest they do with Joseph?

   f. Now briefly summarize what occurs in this paragraph.

3. Now, let's move on to Genesis 37:25-28. Read this paragraph and then complete the following:

    a. Who are the main characters? List them and give a brief description of their roles.

    b. Mark the key words you marked in previous paragraphs and references to killing Joseph such as *shedding his blood* with a black tombstone ▉. (Add this to your bookmark.) Also don't forget to mark geographical locations.

      c. Briefly summarize what occurs in this paragraph.

4. Finally read Genesis 37:29-36.

    a. Did you notice how often Joseph's tunic is mentioned? Mark it as a key word throughout the chapter. Ask the 5 W and H questions to get an idea of what this tunic meant to Jacob. List your observations below.

      b. Mark key words from your bookmark; look for geographical references.

c.      List what you learn about Reuben in this paragraph. How do Judah and Reuben **distinguish** themselves in this incident?

d.  Now summarize this paragraph in one or two sentences.

e.  Finally, at the beginning of your Observation Worksheets record where Joseph is as the chapter opens and at the end where he is as the chapter closes.

f.  Note Jacob's status at the beginning of the chapter and at the end..

g.  Record a theme for Genesis 37 on the "Genesis At A Glance" chart in the Appendix.

> At the end of your study, you will have a handy summary of this portion of Genesis.

> "For whatever was written in earlier times was written for our instruction, so that through perseverance and the encouragement of the Scriptures we might have hope."
> – Romans 15:4

5.  This chapter gives you a historical account of Jacob's sons and serves another purpose. Read Romans 15:4 in the pull-out box. Consider how this chapter can instruct you in similar situations: cause you to persevere, encourage you, warn you, and make you aware of hope. Reading

about others in similar situations and their dependencies on God (good or bad), helps you evaluate where you are and where you're headed.

For instance, has there been favoritism in your family? Have you dealt with jealousy? Have family members ever ganged up on you? Do you see yourself in any of these characters? Can you relate to Joseph, Reuben, Judah? Are you like Joseph's brothers, eaten up with jealousy and unable to talk to a sibling decently, kindly? Has your jealousy turned to hatred? Is there murder in your heart?

If you and/or others you know relate to this situation, then you want to pay careful attention to the chapters ahead. Take a moment now to pray. Consider writing a prayer to God and tell Him what you want to learn.

Record practical insights you gained from your observations of this chapter.

# LESSON FOUR

Genesis 37 opens with the phrase, "These are the records of the generations of Jacob." The phrase "These are the records of the generations" first occurs in Genesis 2:4, the New American Standard Bible translating it, "This is *the account of the heavens and the earth...*" The phrase can be translated: *These are the generations of the heavens and the earth* (c.f. Genesis 5:1; 6:9; 10:1; 11:10,27; 25:12; 25:19; 36:1,9; and 37:2).

In Genesis 37, we see God focusing first on Jacob's son Joseph. Then in Genesis 38, He directs our attention to another son of Jacob.

1. Read Genesis 38 and note the main characters. List them below in order of their importance.

2. Now observe Genesis 38 the same way you did Genesis 37.

    a. Mark key repeated words.

    b. Double underline every geographical location.

    c. Mark time references with a green clock like this: ⏰ .

    d. Watch for references to the *Lord* in this chapter. What do you learn about God? It is so helpful to keep a journal on God as you study the Word of God; it's a real faith builder. Your "Journal on God" is located in the Appendix. Every time you come across a new insight on God, record the book, chapter, and verse, and what you learn about Him. The journal will then become a wonderful aid to worship – because true worship is acknowledging His worth and praising Him for it.

3. Although there is no record of the Law at this point in Israel's history of Israel,[1] it's apparent from the text that God revealed the duty of brothers-in-law (Genesis 38:8) that was later recorded in the Law.

    Read the following scriptures and record what they say about carrying on the bloodline of a family member. As you look at these passages, you will see how long this custom of the law continued.

---

[1] God gave the Law 430 years after the Abrahamic Covenant, when the children of Israel came out of Egypt (Genesis 15:12-17; Galatians 3:16-17).

4. Read the following verse and note key people in the genealogy of Jesus the Messiah. Now, isn't it exciting to see the hand of God in this event in Judah's life?

5.    Finally write out the Genesis 38 theme and record it on the "Genesis At A Glance" chart.

Isn't it encouraging to know that God can bring something wonderful from circumstances like these!?! No matter what has happened in your past, God is willing and able to use you to bring glory to His name. Submit yourself to Him and trust Him to use *your* weaknesses to show <u>Himself</u> strong!

# LESSON FIVE

1. Your assignment for today is simple – observe Genesis 39 as you have previous chapters and mark the text.

   a. Also mark *blessing* (*blessed*) in pink and *sin* in brown. Although *sin* is not repeated in the chapter, it's always good to mark it when you come across it in your Bible and consistently so it will be easy to find. Mark synonyms like *iniquity* and *transgression* the same way. Add these to your keyword bookmark.

   b. Also mark *Hebrew* with a blue Star of David ✡. This is the second time the word is used in the Bible. It first occurs in Genesis 14:13. Add it to your key word bookmark.

   c. List in the margin of your Observation Worksheets all you learn about *Joseph*. When you finish, reflect on these things. Beyond his physical appearance, do you admire, respect, or desire to **imitate** any other qualities of his?

2. Now put yourself in Joseph's place. How would you feel if you were him at the end of this chapter? How would you react if this happened to you? How would you feel about God? How would you respond to Him? Write out your answer.

3. Record your Genesis 39 theme on the "Genesis At A Glance" chart.

# LESSON SIX

1. Think about what you observed in Genesis 39. Read the chapter one more time and then answer the following questions:

   a. Was Joseph's response typical in today's **moral culture**? Explain your answer.

   b. Would it have been a sin for Joseph to have sexual relations with Mrs. Potiphar? Why? Can you support your answer from the Bible? What scriptures can you use to show God's standard?

   c. Now look up the following scriptures and record what they teach about sex outside of marriage and its consequences.

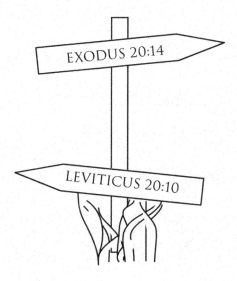

EXODUS 20:14

LEVITICUS 20:10

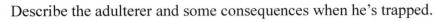
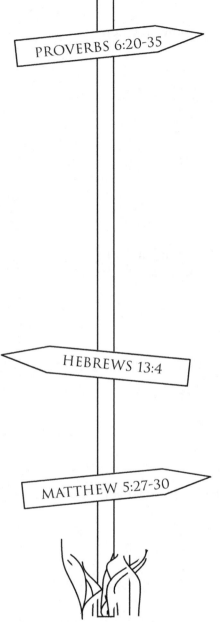

Describe the adulterer and some consequences when he's trapped.

PROVERBS 6:20-35

HEBREWS 13:4

MATTHEW 5:27-30

If you want to know more, look up the following passages and note what they teach about sex outside marriage. If you are not familiar with these passages, write them somewhere in your Bible for future reference so you can share them with others.

- Deuteronomy 22:13-30
- Job 31:1, 9-12
- Proverbs 5:1-23; 7:1-27
- Ephesians 5:5-6
- 1 Thessalonians 4:3-8
- Revelation 21:8

**THE MORE YOU KNOW...**

2. Most people in Joseph's position question God. If he honored God, why didn't God watch over him? Isn't God **obligated** to do so? Why did something bad happen to someone doing right? Is God fair? How would you answer this? Answer the question as if you were sitting in the prison with Joseph and *he* asked *you* why he was there.

Have you ever wondered why bad things happen to people? Maybe you have wondered why bad things have happened in your life when you were obedient and made the right choices. Keep studying! You will find answers as you look at Joseph's life.

## ENRICHMENT WORDS:

**Animosity** – ill will; resentment; active hostility.

**Culture** – customary beliefs and social norms of a race, religion, country, or other social group.

**Distinguish** – separate; differentiate.

**Imitate** – follow a pattern, model, or example.

**Investigate** – closely examine and systematically ask.

**Jealousy** – hostility toward a favored person or competitor.

**Moral** – of or relating to principles of right and wrong.

**Obligated** – bound legally or morally.

**Restoration** – a bringing back to a former position or condition.

**Rival** – a competitor.

**Strife** – bitter, sometimes violent conflict.

# From the Pit to the Palace

Have you ever wondered why God doesn't intervene in tragedies? How can He *be* love, yet allow pain? While you may not understand the reasons God does what He does *in this life*, His Word offers encouragement, healing, and assurance that He is with you and working in the midst of sin, pain, and hardship.

As you study Genesis 40 and 41 this week, you will learn a lot about God's ways. It's going to be another great week of looking at the spiritual side of life and seeing how your understanding of spiritual things influences how you live. Is true spirituality **mystical** thoughts and emotional experiences? How down-to-earth is your relationship to God?

Begin with prayer. Read the one below and add your personal requests.

## ONE ON ONE:

*God, I want to know truth – understand You as You really are. I don't want to trust my own ways or feelings only to find myself far from your truth. Lead me to understand Your Word. Many people say truth is relative to man. What do You say, Father? Surely, You determine what is true. Open my spiritual eyes and lead me in Your ways. Then, give me strength to follow You. I believe You are here with me now and You have heard my heart's cry. Thank You for teaching me through Your Word.*

# LESSON ONE

1. Read Genesis 39:19 through chapter 40, watching how events unfold. Don't rush.

2. Now look at the text in more detail. You know where Joseph is and why. Observe Genesis 40 and record the main events in the margins of your Observation Worksheets.

    a. Mark *dream* with a cloud and *Hebrew* with a blue Star of David ✡.

    b.  Add these words to your key word bookmark.

    c. Mark references to time and geographical locations.

    d. Observe what you learn about God and record it in the "Journal on God" you began last week.

# LESSON TWO

1.  Read Genesis 40:20 through Genesis 41. Note where Joseph is as chapter 41 begins and where he is when the chapter closes. Record this next to the first and last verses on your Observation Worksheets.

2.  Record the main events and topics in these chapters in the margins of your Observation Worksheets.

> Listing key events in the margins of the text will serve as quick references to the main events and topics covered in the chapter. For example, next to Genesis 41:14 you could write, "Joseph brought from prison to Pharaoh."

3.  Now note Joseph's age in the margin. From this you can calculate the time interval between Genesis 37 and Genesis 41.

    a.  How old is Joseph in Genesis 37 and 41?

    b.  How long has Joseph been away from his family?

# LESSON THREE

1. Now, look closer at Genesis 41. Read the chapter and mark key words, geographical locations, and references to time.

   a. Add *famine* to your key word bookmark and mark it in the chapter.

   b.  Watch what you learn about God. There are some interesting things to note in your journal.

   c. Draw Pharoah's two dreams in the space below.

2. Think about what you learned about Joseph in Unit One and the last two lessons. How did Joseph conduct himself in the midst of each situation he faced? What does he say about God? How does he behave, respond, answer his superiors, relate to others, etc.?

   Record your insights on the chart on page 38. Then look at your life. Where are you encouraged? What can you learn from Joseph's life that will help you become more Christlike? What do you need to remember or start doing?

| INSIGHTS ON JOSEPH'S LIFE | INSIGHTS ON MY LIFE |
|---|---|
|  |  |

3. It's so apparent, isn't it, that God *does* notice your behavior. Then in His righteousness and justice, and according to His timing, He moves on your behalf. What is your prayer in light of the last assignment? Do you need to ask God forgiveness for not trusting Him. Do you need to ask Him to help you put into practice the truths you learned? Write it out below.

4. Record main themes for Genesis 40 and 41 on the "Genesis At A Glance" chart.

# LESSON FOUR

Too often people know one side of God – the side others taught them. Some see God as only vengeful and full of wrath, ready to punish anyone who steps out of line. Others believe only what they want God to be: merciful, loving, accepting of anyone and anything. Who is right? Is there more than one side to God? Does it matter what you believe about God's character?

1. Begin the day by reviewing your "Journal on God." If you have any questions about God, write them below.

2. When you reviewed your insights on God, did it surprise you to see that God caused the famine? If you missed that, read Genesis 41:28, 32. Then look up the following verses and note other things God does. Also record reasons why God does these things, if reasons are given.

   Check the context for each reference and note who is speaking and about what.

HAGGAI 1:9-11

What do you think now? These scriptures contradict the idea of a distant God who just loves, comforts, and accepts everyone. How do you react to this information? Does it frighten you? humble you? make you want to stand in awe of Him?

# LESSON FIVE

*U-2, Lesson 5, Chapters 40-41*

1. What kind of God is this who creates adversity as well as well-being? You need to know to understand and trust Him. Daniel 11:32b says that the people who know their God will display strength and take action. Understanding God's **attributes** will give you strength and courage for the days ahead – this will be your task for this lesson.

   God's character is a composite of His attributes. The attributes are not a part of His being, they are His being. God is love and also wrathful, but these do not **contradict** each other; they make God who He is.

   Read through the list below of God's attributes and look up the scriptures that show them. Record attributes in the margin of your Bible and color them in a special way to easily spot them. You may also want to put this list in your "Journal on God."

   As you look up each attribute, determine if and how it applies to God's dealings with Joseph. Note your insights under the appropriate attribute.

   And lastly, remember that each member of the Godhead – the Father, Son, and Holy Spirit – has the same attributes.

## THE NATURAL ATTRIBUTES OF GOD – WHAT HE IS

**Omniscient** – God knows all: Himself and His creation – past, present, and future. (Job 37:16; Psalm 139:1-6)

**Omnipotent** – God possesses all power. He causes everything He has decided to cause. (2 Kings 19:25; Job 38:4–40:2; Job 42:2; Psalm 33:6-9; 115:3; Isaiah 14:24, 27; 46:11)

**Omnipresent** – God is present everywhere, in all the universe, at all times, in the totality of His character. (Proverbs 15:3; Jeremiah 23:23-24)

© 2008 Precept Ministries International                                                                41

**Eternal** – God has no beginning, and He has no end. He is timeless and in fact, the cause of time. (Deuteronomy 32:40; Revelation 1:8; Isaiah 57:15)

**Immutable** – God is always the same in His nature, character, and will. He does not and cannot change. (Psalm 102:25-27; Malachi 3:6; and Hebrews 13:8)

**Incomprehensible** – He is beyond full understanding. His ways, character, and acts are higher than man's. Man only understands what God reveals of Himself, His ways, and His purposes. (Job 11:7; Romans 11:33)

**Self-existent** – God depends on nothing for His existence. He exists in Himself. Before time, nothing but God existed. He added nothing to Himself by creation. (John 1:1-3; Exodus 3:14 –"AM" is translated *hayah*, which means to exist; John 5:26)

**Self-sufficient** – God acts without assistance. (Psalm 50:7-12; Acts 17:24-25; Romans 11:36)

**Infinite** – God has no limits or bounds in His dominion. (1 Kings 8:27; Psalm 145:3)

**Transcendent** – God is above His creation; He exists apart from and as if there were no creation. (Isaiah 43:10; 55:8-9)

**Sovereign** – God totally, supremely, and preeminently rules over all His creation. No person or thing escapes His control and foreknown plan! (Psalm 103:19; Daniel 4:34-35; Isaiah 40:23; 46:8-11)

## GOD'S MORAL ATTRIBUTES WHICH SHOW HIS RELATIONSHIP TO HIS CREATION

**Holy** – God is morally excellent and perfectly pure. (Leviticus 19:2; Job 34:10; Isaiah 47:4; and Isaiah 57:15)

**Gracious** – God loves unconditionally. (Exodus 34:6-7; 2 Chronicles 30:9; Luke 2:40; 2 Corinthians 12:9)

**Righteous** – God is always right. He always does the right thing. His actions are always consistent with His love. (Deuteronomy 32:4; Psalm 119:142)

**Just** – God is fair in all of His actions. Whether He deals with man, angels, or demons, He rewards righteousness and punishes sin. His decrees are absolutely just. (Psalm 89:14; Numbers 14:18; 23:19; Romans 9:14)

**Merciful** – God is compassionate even toward those who oppose His will in their pursuit of their own way. NOTE: The NASB translates mercy as "lovingkindness" and "compassion." (Psalm 62:12; 86:15; 106:44-45; Lamentations 3:22-23, Psalm 145:8-9)

**Longsuffering/Patient** – God's righteous anger kindles slowly against those who disobey. (Numbers 14:18 [slow to anger, NASB]; 2 Peter 3:9 [patient, NASB])

**Wise** – God's intelligence includes perfectly fitting together means and ends. (Isaiah 40:28; Daniel 2:20)

**Loving** – God gives Himself to His people, even to the extent of sacrificing His Son. His love causes Him to desire their highest good. This love is not based on their worth, response, or merit. (Romans 5:8; 1 John 4:8; Ephesians 3:17-19)

**Good** – God gives to others, not according to what they deserve but according to His will and kindness. (2 Chronicles 5:13; Psalm 106:1)

**Wrathful** – God hates all unrighteousness and immutably wills to punish it. Whatever is inconsistent with His holy standard is ultimately atoned for or consumed. (Romans 1:18; John 3:36; 2 Chronicles 19:2; Colossians 3:5-6; Revelation 15:7)

**Truthful** – All God says is objective reality whether His creatures believe or not. God cannot lie. (Numbers 23:19; John 17:17; Titus 1:2; Hebrews 6:18)

**Faithful** – God is always true to His promises. He never repents of His promises to bless or judge. Since He cannot lie, He always does what He has spoken. (Deuteronomy 7:9; Romans 11:29; 2 Timothy 2:13)

**Jealous** – God does not share what is rightfully His (e.g. worship, glory) with any creature. (Exodus 34:14; Isaiah 42:8)

## "WHO GOD IS" PROJECT

For this project you will need:

*Newspapers, magazines, Internet*

*Posterboard*

1. Write a summary including definitions of two or three attributes with supporting scriptures.

2. Write a paragraph explaining how you have seen each attribute work your life or in someone else's. (You may need to interview family members and friends.) You can use newspaper, magazine and Internet articles that show attributes at work.

3. Make a posterboard with pictures or drawings that represent the attributes you researched. Be creative and detailed!

---

The immutable God never acts contrary to Himself!

What peace, what security, what confidence this should bring to your heart and mind. Anytime you come across a biblical doctrine or situation you don't fully understand, run to the shelter of God's character and rest quietly in these solid, eternal truths.

Rest, and order your affairs accordingly. Follow Joseph's example.

## ENRICHMENT WORDS:

**Attributes** – inherent characteristics.

**Contradict** – to affirm the opposite, deny.

**Mystical** – unintelligible, non-rational.

# Feast or Famine

You've seen images of children in other countries starving and malnourished. Is that happening where you are today?

Maybe **famine** in your country is not physical but spiritual. Amos 8:11 speaks of famine "for hearing the words of the Lord." Is there a hunger for hearing the words of the Lord in your country, community, school, among your friends, or even in your heart? Spiritually speaking, are you like those suffering from lack of food... malnourished and diseased?

> *"Behold, days are coming,"*
> *declares the Lord God, "When*
> *I will send a famine on the*
> *land, Not a famine for bread*
> *or a thirst for water, but*
> *rather for hearing the words*
> *of the Lord."*
>
> *– Amos 8:11*

Many people have several copies of God's Word – essentially a permanent supply of food – yet are starving. Do you take the bread of God to nourish yourself? Don't grow tired of feeding on the words of the Lord! His words are relevant – you need them to satisfy your soul's deep hunger for truth and life.

You have an awesome study of Genesis 42-47 this week. You are about to read an incredible story rich with valuable precepts for life that will enrich your knowledge of and confidence in the One who rules from heaven over the affairs of man – the One who has numbered the hairs of your head, the One who cares for you so deeply that He promises to provide all your needs if you seek first His kingdom and righteousness.

Read the following prayer. Remember your goal in studying God's Word is to KNOW HIM so you will live differently from the world. Tell God this is the desire of your heart.

ONE ON ONE:

*Father, thank You for all I have learned about You. Thank You for who You are and what You have revealed to me in Your Word so I could know You brought me into existence and formed me out of "Your good pleasure" (Revelation 4). Thank You that You never change so I know that I can trust You. Thank You for Your love, mercy, and grace.*

*Father, as I study Your Word, I pray that Your Holy Spirit will remind me to guard my study time and not let **temporal** and worthless things keep me from knowing You.*

*You know what is on my heart; You know my past, present, and future. You know what I need. Meet that need through the bread of heaven, Your Son and Your Word. Father, feed me your Word. Nourish me from it. Strengthen me so I will live satisfied by You alone!*

*I ask this in the matchless name of Jesus Christ who gives me access to Your sovereign throne. Amen.*

1.  Begin today's lesson by reading Genesis 41:50-42:38.

    a.  Record the names of Joseph's sons and *why* he so named them. If you have a New Inductive Study Bible (NISB), you will find meanings of their names in the margin.

    b.  Mark time references and then note when Genesis 41:53-57 occurred relative to the interpretation of Pharaoh's dreams.

    c.  What is about to begin? Record this in the margin of your Observation Worksheet.

2.  Now read Genesis 42 again and complete the following observations.

    a.  Mark references that tell you when and where things are occurring.

    b. Mark references to money with a dollar sign: $.

    c.  Mark key words *famine*, *die*, and *sin* as you have previously.

    d.  Don't miss expressions of emotion in this chapter! Mark *weep*, *wept*, and its synonyms with a blue tear like this 𝟺. Do this throughout your study.

    e.  Finally, record new things you learn about God in your journal.

3.  Genesis 42:9 says Joseph remembered his dreams about his brothers. What do you think provoked this memory? Underline or mark in a distinctive way what Joseph's brothers do in Genesis 42:6. This action will become a key word that you should mark throughout this study (add it to your key word bookmark).

4.  Note main events covered in this chapter and record them in the margins of your Observation Worksheets.

5.  Record a theme for Genesis 42 on the "Genesis At A Glance" chart.

6. Now, pause and think about what happened with Joseph's brothers in Genesis 42:21-24, 28. Have you ever been in a similar circumstance? What do you see here? What do you learn without being directly told? Are there lessons for life here? What can you apply to your life? Record your insights below.

1. Read Genesis 42:1-5 and Genesis 43:1-2. Note why Joseph's brothers went to Egypt on two difference occasions.

2. Do a **topical** study on the subject of famines to see what Scripture teaches about them and why a sovereign God causes them.

   a. Look up the following scriptures. Don't be overwhelmed with the details. Look for why the famine came, who made it happen, who it affected, who God preserved in it, and what resulted. Examine the text as you have done before in the light of the 5 Ws and H.

   b. As you read these passages mark *famine* as you have before. Also, see if any references refer to the famine mentioned in Genesis 41-43.

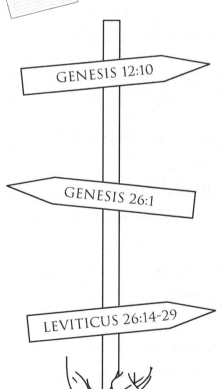

GENESIS 12:10

GENESIS 26:1

LEVITICUS 26:14-29

(This passage is printed for you on the next two pages. Mark *obey* and then record below what you learn about famine and obedience.)

## LEVITICUS 26:14-29

14 'But if you do not obey Me and do not carry out all these commandments,

15 if, instead, you reject My statutes, and if your soul abhors My ordinances so as not to carry out all My commandments, and so break My covenant,

16 I, in turn, will do this to you: I will appoint over you a sudden terror, consumption and fever that will waste away the eyes and cause the soul to pine away; also, you will sow your seed uselessly, for your enemies will eat it up.

17 'I will set My face against you so that you will be struck down before your enemies; and those who hate you will rule over you, and you will flee when no one is pursuing you.

18 'If also after these things you do not obey Me, then I will punish you seven times more for your sins.

19 'I will also break down your pride of power; I will also make your sky like iron and your earth like bronze.

20 'Your strength will be spent uselessly, for your land will not yield its produce and the trees of the land will not yield their fruit.

21 'If then, you act with hostility against Me and are unwilling to obey Me, I will increase the plague on you seven times according to your sins.

22 'I will let loose among you the beasts of the field, which will bereave you of your children and destroy your cattle and reduce your number so that your roads lie deserted.

23 'And if by these things you are not turned to Me, but act with hostility against Me,

24 then I will act with hostility against you; and I, even I, will strike you seven times for your sins.

25 'I will also bring upon you a sword which will execute vengeance for the covenant; and when you gather together into your cities, I will send pestilence among you, so that you shall be delivered into enemy hands.

26 'When I break your staff of bread, ten women will bake your bread in one oven, and they will bring back your bread in rationed amounts, so that you will eat and not be satisfied.

27    'Yet if in spite of this you do not obey Me, but act with hostility against Me,

28    then I will act with wrathful hostility against you, and I, even I, will punish you
seven times for your sins.

29    'Further, you will eat the flesh of your sons and the flesh of your daughters you
will eat.

2 CHRONICLES 6:13, 26-31

ISAIAH 3:1-8

JEREMIAH 14:11-18

JEREMIAH 29:17-19

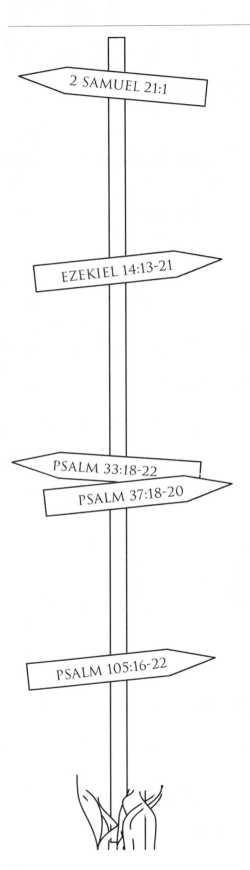

2 SAMUEL 21:1

EZEKIEL 14:13-21

PSALM 33:18-22

PSALM 37:18-20

PSALM 105:16-22

3.  Wow! The Word of God contains a lot of information about famines, doesn't it? Answer the following questions to summarize what you learned.

    a.  Why does God cause famines?

    b.  Who does God affect by famines? Who does He preserve?

    c.  What does God accomplish with famines? Keep this in mind as you interpret the ones in Joseph's time.

4.  Since famines will come in the future, what have you learned from these passages that you can apply to yourself and tell others?

    a.  What protects us in famines?

b.  When Christians hear about **impending** disasters, many say, "I'm going to trust God" and do nothing to prepare. What do you think about that? What did Joseph think *and do*?

---

Are you anchored?

Are you deeply rooted?

If you haven't experienced them already, life's storms are coming. If the sun is out now, if life is great and you only see blue skies above you, praise God! But are you ready for the wind and rain coming? Trials, tribulations, stuggles and suffering are down the road. Do you know where to run when it comes?

Reconsider this story of a man who lived long ago, whose faith and wisdom greatly applies to your life today. If you're in a situation and don't know what to do... think about what God taught you through Joseph's experiences.

---

# LESSON THREE

1.  Read and mark Genesis 43. Remember to mark *Hebrew*(s) and when Joseph's brothers *bowed* before him (as in Lesson One).

2.  Now observe what you learn about God and how He is to be feared. As you examine the text, ask yourself how you would have handled these situations compared with the response and attitude of those in this chapter. Jot down insights below.

3.  In the margins of your Observation Worksheets, record the main events in this chapter. Then draw a picture below representing each event.

# LESSON FOUR

1. Read and mark Genesis 44. Record the main events of this chapter as before. Also mark references to *sin* (*iniquity*).

2. What iniquity do you think Judah is referring to in Genesis 44:16? What insight does this give you into the consequences of sin?

3. Record themes for Genesis 43 and 44 on the "Genesis At A Glance" chart.

Doesn't it help to slow down and observe the text? God will honor your diligence and give you opportunities to share what you learned with others. The topic certainly is relevant. People need godly heroes of the faith – those who study the Word of God and live by it. Be one!

# LESSON FIVE

1. Genesis 45 is great! You'll enjoy reading this chapter and marking key words. Do your usual thing... mark key words and record main events in the margins of your Observation Worksheets.

   a. Pay special attention to time phrases because they will help you discover Joseph's age.

   b. Observe expressions of emotion in this chapter, which reveal the humanity of the characters. Mark references to *weeping* as you did before. (Put yourself in the place of those who weep.)

   c. Record a theme for Genesis 45 on the "Genesis At A Glance" chart.

2. Now look for personal application from this historical account.

   a. Do you have the same attitude Joseph had toward difficult situations? How so or not?

   b. How would you respond to brothers who did what Joseph's did?

c.  What has God taught you through today's study?

> You may have been swept by storms already. You've related to Joseph's hardships!
>
> You may have experienced the deepest pain and suffering. You may also be well acquainted with bitterness, jealousy and strife within your family, church, community, or school. Whatever the offense, is forgiveness possible?
>
> You may have experienced searing pain brought on by your own sin, regret and remorse your constant companions.
>
> You may have been wronged, blamed, lied to, abandoned.
>
> What have you learned from Joseph's life that you can apply to these situations? What does God want you to KNOW?
>
> What is God telling you to DO?

# LESSON SIX

1. Read Genesis 46-47, marking and recording your observations. From this point on, mark references to *blessed* and *blessing*. Add them to your key word bookmark.

2. Record your insights on God in your journal.

3. List your insights on Joseph's dealings with those who came to buy grain.

4. Record themes for Genesis 46 and 47 on the "Genesis At A Glance" chart.

5. What did God record in Genesis 46:8-27? Why do you think He did this? Read the verses in the signs below and then write out your answer.

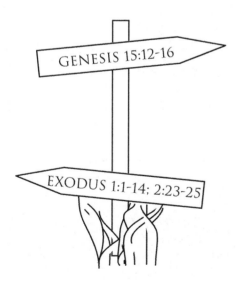

GENESIS 15:12-16

EXODUS 1:1-14; 2:23-25

6. Do you think famine plays a role in this? Support your answer.

7. Finally, read the introduction to this unit and think about it.

   a. Do you see parallels between Amos 8:11 and what Joseph did?

   b. If a famine for the Word of God comes, have you stored enough grain to feed yourself and others?

One more unit to complete your study!

We commend you for your discipline. Doesn't it give you a sense of accomplishment? After all, you are doing what you should be doing – studying to show yourself approved to God, a workman that does not need to be ashamed. You're learning how to handle the Word accurately. Press on. The last unit will be so rich. Don't let anything keep you from it!

ENRICHMENT WORDS:

**Famine** – an extreme scarcity of food.

**Impending** – happening soon.

**Temporal** – not permanent, not eternal.

# Trust in Tragedy

Forgiveness. What does it mean? Are you supposed to forgive those who cause pain? What if you can't forgive? What if you choose not to forgive?

Do you know why forgiveness is important? Do you realize it sets us free? Joseph learned this lesson when he confronted the brothers who sold him into a life of slavery. What did Joseph know that gave him the desire and ability to forgive those who caused him so much pain?

Forgiveness is hard. But God can cause you to forgive the wrong done to you for your good and His glory, just as He did to Joseph.

This final unit of study can be a turning point for you in your walk with the Lord. Pray as you begin, and wait on the Lord.

## ONE ON ONE: PRAYER

*Father, as I begin this final unit, search my heart for sin and reveal it. Send Your Word, save me from sin, and deliver me from distress – from self-destructive things that keep me from saving and rescuing others.*

*Show me how You can use me as you did Joseph. Thank You for his example. Thank You for his response. Thank You for the Holy Spirit – the Enabler, the Helper – indwelling me.*

*Give me wisdom and understanding. Help me grow in the knowledge of*

*You and more and more into Your Son's likeness. May this be evident in my life as others see Him rule me.*

*I ask this in the name of the Son of David from the Tribe of Judah, the Lord Jesus Christ. Amen.*

# LESSON ONE

1.  Begin this unit by reading Acts 7:8-16. It will give you some background to what you covered and an overview of what you are going to study in this unit.

2.  Read Genesis 41:50-52, then read Genesis 47:27–48:22 to put yourself back into the context of Joseph's life.

3.  Now observe Genesis 48 more closely.

    a.    Read and mark the text as you have previously. Mark *blessing* with a pink cloud.

    b.  Also mark *Ephraim* and *Manasseh* in distinct ways.

    c.  Give special attention to what Jacob says about God when he blesses Joseph.

4.  Evaluate the events of this chapter by answering the following questions.

    a.  What happened when Jacob blessed Joseph's sons?

    b.  Does this remind you of Jacob's life at all? How?

    c.  What determines the outcome of your life – tradition, culture, society, or God?

# LESSON TWO

When Jacob blesses Joseph, he speaks of "the God before whom my fathers Abraham and Isaac walked...." (Genesis 48:15). What a **legacy**!

1.  What does walking with God mean? Joseph has been on a journey of discovering God that included some pretty interesting and intense places – a pit, slavery, prison, and a palace! He began when he was just 17 years old. You too can take a bold stand for the Lord, walk with Him, and stand firm in tough circumstances. It's not always easy but think ahead and put yourself in Jacob's shoes. Wouldn't you like to have a legacy of walking with the Lord?

    Next to each of the following cross-references, record what you learn about walking with God. See if the text tells you who walked with God or who God **exhorted** to walk with Him, when or how they walked with God, and what the result was.

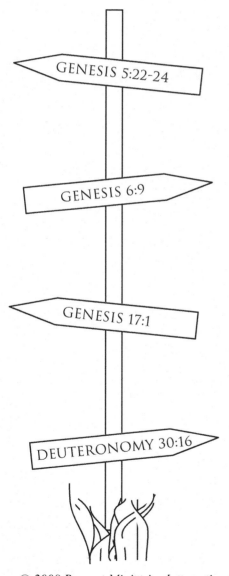

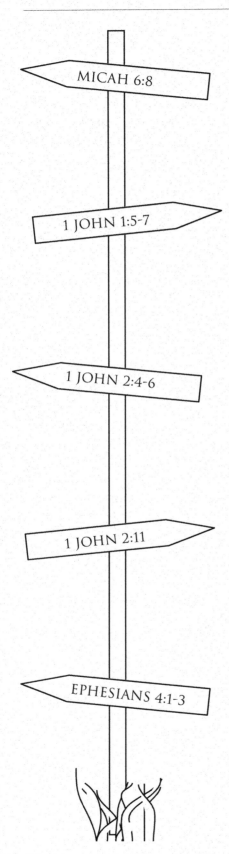

MICAH 6:8

1 JOHN 1:5-7

1 JOHN 2:4-6

1 JOHN 2:11

EPHESIANS 4:1-3

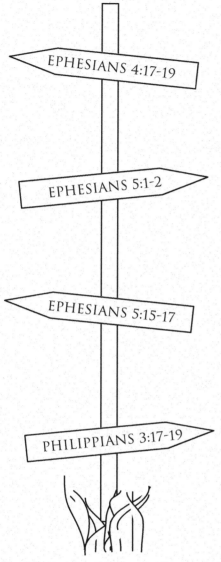

2.  Now, what have you learned about walking with God that you can apply to your life? Can you list at least five things? After recording them below, consider copying them on a small note and putting it on your bathroom mirror or in the front of your Bible so you can look at it every day.

3.     Record the main theme of Genesis 48 on the "Genesis At A Glance" chart.

## "THE PIT, SLAVERY, PRISON, AND PALACE" PROJECT

For this project you will need:

*A poster board*

Draw these four scenarios – the pit, the slave, the prison, the palace – that Joseph faced on a poster board. Then briefly describe under each drawing what the text says about Joseph in this circumstance and what brought him to this place. For example, under "the pit" you could write: betrayed, hated, plotted against, etc.

Now think about a difficult circumstance in your life and write a brief essay describing how it relates to Joseph's experience. What was your "pit?" Were you enslaved to the circumstance... trapped? And how did God take you to a better place? You may not be all the way through this trial yet. If so, describe your situation and honestly say whether you believe God can take you to a "palace."

*"And we know that God causes all things to work together for good to those who love God, to those who are called according to His purpose." (Romans 8:28 )*

# LESSON THREE

1. You are about to observe an interesting chapter! As you look at Genesis 49:

      a. Mark or highlight each of the sons of Israel in one color to distinguish the beginning of the blessing.

      b. Mark *blessing* as you did before.

      c. Record a theme for Genesis 49 on the "Genesis At A Glance" chart. (The first two verses of Genesis 49 and verse 28 are very important because they summarize the content of the chapter.)

2. Which two sons received the longest blessings?

3. The birthright usually belonged to the firstborn son, regardless of the status of the wife. Look up the verses below and record what they tell you about the birthright: who it was given to and why.

4. Before you leave Genesis 49, record what you observed about Joseph's blessing. Note how many times *blessing* is used in conjunction with Joseph. On the following chart record what you learn about Joseph from observing Genesis 49:22-26; Genesis 41:52; 1 Chronicles 5:2; Deuteronomy 33:13-17.

| WHAT HE WAS LIKE | HOW OTHERS TREATED HIM | HOW HE RESPONDED | HIS REWARD |
|---|---|---|---|
|  |  |  |  |

# LESSON FOUR

1. Do a little research into *Judah*. List what you learn from Genesis 49:8-12 about his person, status, and relationships as Jacob prophesies about the days to come, literally "in the end of the days." By the way, the Hebrew Shiloh means "to whom it belongs." Compare this with 1 Chronicles 5:2.

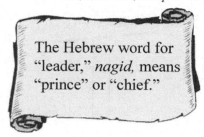

The Hebrew word for "leader," *nagid,* means "prince" or "chief."

## JUDAH
## THE SON OF ISRAEL

| HIS PERSON | HIS STATUS | HIS RELATIONSHIPS |
|---|---|---|
| | | |
| | | |
| | | |

2. Now look at the following verses to see what you learn about Judah and his descendant David, the king of Israel. Watch for indications of the "scepter."

The Hebrew term for "scepter" (NASB) can also be translated "law-giver" (KJV).

PSALM 60:7

ISAIAH 9:6-7

Watch for "government" or indications of governing.

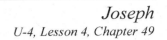
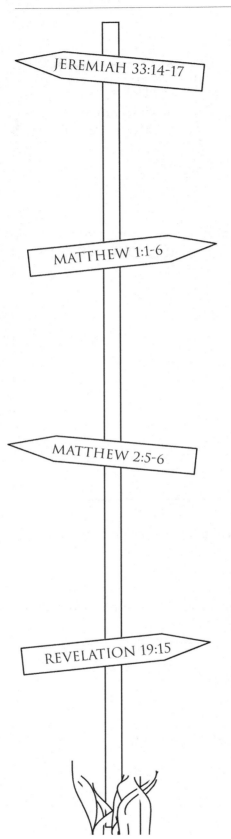

Note who is singled out among his brothers in Jesus' genealogy (Matthew 1:2).

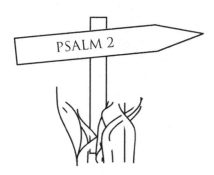

Close today's lesson with this benediction.

3. Someday every knee will bow and every tongue will declare what God has already declared in His Word: Jesus Christ is Lord. Although many refuse Him and walk the broad path to destruction, surely you won't follow them, will you? If you haven't received Jesus Christ, hopefully you'll do it now. If so, simply record your commitment below.

You have come to the last chapter in Genesis – the end of Joseph's story and the beginning of the history of Israel, a company of 70 people who went to Egypt.

Today's study will be rich, so ask God to prepare your heart.

1. Read Genesis 49:29-50:26. What three primary events are covered in Genesis 50? List them in the margins of your Observation Worksheets.

2. Record a theme for Genesis 50 on the "At A Glance" chart.

3. Now read Genesis 50 again and mark references to:

   a. Joseph's brothers *bowing* before him (as you did previously).

   b. *dying* with a tombstone like this ⌂ and *weeping* with a blue teardrop.

   c. *transgression* in brown.

   d. *forgive* with a blue cloud and *afraid* with a brown box.

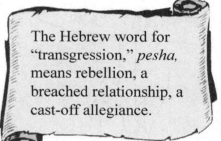

The Hebrew word for "transgression," *pesha,* means rebellion, a breached relationship, a cast-off allegiance.

   e. time phrases and locations. Trace the procession from Egypt to Jacob's burial place on your map. Observe who went to this burial. Mark every reference to *bury* with a shovel.

4. What were the brothers concerned about after their father died?

5. Spend a few minutes looking at what happened with Joseph and his brothers after Jacob died.

   a. How did Joseph respond to his brothers' concern?

b. List everything you observe about Joseph's response and attitude toward his brothers and why he believed God allowed the events in his life.

c. Read the verses in the sign below. How do they apply to Joseph's situation and yours?

ROMANS 8:28-30

Although Joseph lived thousands of years ago, his story could very well be the plot of a TV drama or movie today. Put yourself in his shoes. What would you have done? When people have hurt you, how have you responded?

6. Now look at Joseph's treatment of his brothers and see what God says about forgiveness. **Bitterness** can cripple you for life and defile others until God uproots it. The one who refuses to forgive becomes **captive** to the offender.

As you read the following scriptures, note what they teach about forgiveness. Question each passage with the 5Ws and H. Note who should forgive, what is forgiven, when, where, why, and how. Identify what happens if forgiveness is not extended.

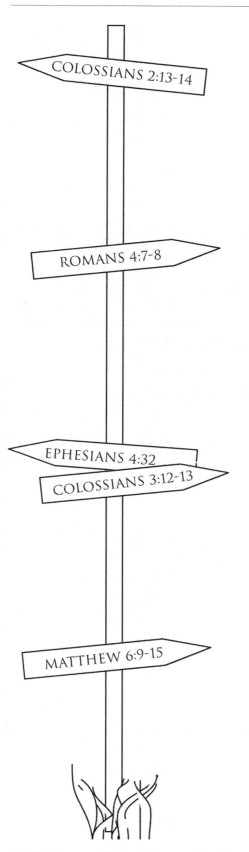

COLOSSIANS 2:13-14

ROMANS 4:7-8

EPHESIANS 4:32

COLOSSIANS 3:12-13

MATTHEW 6:9-15

7.  Is there anyone you need to forgive? If so, write their name(s) down in the box below with what you need to forgive. Then do it!

    Remember that forgiving someone doesn't always mean you'll forget what the offender did, the relationship will be restored, or the offender will go unpunished. Some of these aren't possible if the offender does not submit to God, acknowledge his grave sin, repent (change his mind), and receive Christ. Forgive means "to send away" their offense. You no longer "get even" or retaliate.

| WHO I NEED TO FORGIVE | WHAT I NEED TO FORGIVE |
|---|---|
| | |

8.  Think about Genesis 50:20 in respect to evil done to you. How can God use that in your life to preserve or help others?

9.  Finally, let's look at Genesis 50:24-25.

    a.  What did Joseph prophesy to his brothers?

    b.  Compare this to Genesis 15:13-16.

        1)  What will happen to the sons of Jacob?

        2)  For how long?

        3)  Then what?

        4)  How does God relate to the events?

Shiloh is coming – One who deserves honor, power, glory, and dominion forever and ever. He is coming and "His reward is with Him" to give us according to our deeds.

Joseph left the sons of Israel a promise of hope – even as the Lord Jesus Christ left us with this one: He will return. Until then, He says, "Occupy till I come." Do the Lord's work, labor diligently in His field "white for harvest."

Be "doers of the Word" as well as "hearers." Continue to study "to present yourself approved to God as a workman who does not need to be ashamed, handling accurately the word of truth" (2 Timothy 2:15).

## ENRICHMENT WORDS:

**Bitterness** – intense antagonism, hostility.

**Captive** – held under the control of another.

**Exhort** – urge strongly.

**Legacy** – something transmitted by or received from an ancestor or predecessor or from the past; fame (good reputation) or infamy (bad reputation) passed on to subsequent generations.

# APPENDIX

*Joseph*

CONTENTS:

- GENESIS 37-50 OBSERVATION WORKSHEETS

- GENESIS 1-50 AT A GLANCE CHART

- MAPS

- MY JOURNAL ON GOD

- ABOUT PRECEPT MINISTRIES INTERNATIONAL

# GENESIS 37
## Observation Worksheet

Chapter Theme _____

1   Now Jacob lived in the land where his father had sojourned, in the land of Canaan.

2   These are *the records* of the generations of Jacob.

Joseph, when seventeen years of age, was pasturing the flock with his brothers while he was *still* a youth, along with the sons of Bilhah and the sons of Zilpah, his father's wives. And Joseph brought back a bad report about them to their father.

3   Now Israel loved Joseph more than all his sons, because he was the son of his old age; and he made him a varicolored tunic.

4   His brothers saw that their father loved him more than all his brothers; and *so* they hated him and could not speak to him on friendly terms.

5   Then Joseph had a dream, and when he told it to his brothers, they hated him even more.

6   He said to them, "Please listen to this dream which I have had;

7   for behold, we were binding sheaves in the field, and lo, my sheaf rose up and also stood erect; and behold, your sheaves gathered around and bowed down to my sheaf."

8   Then his brothers said to him, "Are you actually going to reign over us? Or are you really going to rule over us?" So they hated him even more for his dreams and for his words.

9   Now he had still another dream, and related it to his brothers, and said, "Lo, I have had still another dream; and behold, the sun and the moon and eleven stars were bowing down to me."

10 He related *it* to his father and to his brothers; and his father rebuked him and said to him, "What is this dream that you have had? Shall I and your mother and your brothers actually come to bow ourselves down before you to the ground?"

11 His brothers were jealous of him, but his father kept the saying *in mind.*

**12** Then his brothers went to pasture their father's flock in Shechem.

13 Israel said to Joseph, "Are not your brothers pasturing *the flock* in Shechem? Come, and I will send you to them." And he said to him, "I will go."

14 Then he said to him, "Go now and see about the welfare of your brothers and the welfare of the flock, and bring word back to me." So he sent him from the valley of Hebron, and he came to Shechem.

**15** A man found him, and behold, he was wandering in the field; and the man asked him, "What are you looking for?"

16 He said, "I am looking for my brothers; please tell me where they are pasturing *the flock.*"

17 Then the man said, "They have moved from here; for I heard *them* say, 'Let us go to Dothan.'" So Joseph went after his brothers and found them at Dothan.

**18** Then they saw him from a distance and before he came close to them, they plotted against him to put him to death.

19 They said to one another, "Here comes this dreamer!

20 "Now then, come and let us kill him and throw him into one of the pits; and we will say, 'A wild beast devoured him.' Then let us see what will become of his dreams!"

21 But Reuben heard *this* and rescued him out of their hands and said, "Let us not take his life."

22 Reuben further said to them, "Shed no blood. Throw him into this pit that is in the wilderness, but do not lay hands on him"—that he might rescue him out of their hands, to restore him to his father.

23 So it came about, when Joseph reached his brothers, that they stripped Joseph of his tunic, the varicolored tunic that was on him;

24    and they took him and threw him into the pit. Now the pit was empty, without any water in it.

25    Then they sat down to eat a meal. And as they raised their eyes and looked, behold, a caravan of Ishmaelites was coming from Gilead, with their camels bearing aromatic gum and balm and myrrh, on their way to bring *them* down to Egypt.

26    Judah said to his brothers, "What profit is it for us to kill our brother and cover up his blood?

27    "Come and let us sell him to the Ishmaelites and not lay our hands on him, for he is our brother, our *own* flesh." And his brothers listened *to him*.

28    Then some Midianite traders passed by, so they pulled *him* up and lifted Joseph out of the pit, and sold him to the Ishmaelites for twenty *shekels* of silver. Thus they brought Joseph into Egypt.

29    Now Reuben returned to the pit, and behold, Joseph was not in the pit; so he tore his garments.

30    He returned to his brothers and said, "The boy is not *there*; as for me, where am I to go?"

31    So they took Joseph's tunic, and slaughtered a male goat and dipped the tunic in the blood;

32    and they sent the varicolored tunic and brought it to their father and said, "We found this; please examine *it* to *see* whether it is your son's tunic or not."

33    Then he examined it and said, "It is my son's tunic. A wild beast has devoured him; Joseph has surely been torn to pieces!"

34    So Jacob tore his clothes, and put sackcloth on his loins and mourned for his son many days.

35    Then all his sons and all his daughters arose to comfort him, but he refused to be comforted. And he said, "Surely I will go down to Sheol in mourning for my son." So his father wept for him.

36    Meanwhile, the Midianites sold him in Egypt to Potiphar, Pharaoh's officer, the captain of the bodyguard.

# GENESIS 38
## Observation Worksheet

Chapter Theme _____

1    And it came about at that time, that Judah departed from his brothers and visited a certain Adullamite, whose name was Hirah.

2    Judah saw there a daughter of a certain Canaanite whose name was Shua; and he took her and went in to her.

3    So she conceived and bore a son and he named him Er.

4    Then she conceived again and bore a son and named him Onan.

5    She bore still another son and named him Shelah; and it was at Chezib that she bore him.

**6**    Now Judah took a wife for Er his firstborn, and her name *was* Tamar.

7    But Er, Judah's firstborn, was evil in the sight of the Lord, so the Lord took his life.

8    Then Judah said to Onan, "Go in to your brother's wife, and perform your duty as a brother-in-law to her, and raise up offspring for your brother."

9    Onan knew that the offspring would not be his; so when he went in to his brother's wife, he wasted his seed on the ground in order not to give offspring to his brother.

10    But what he did was displeasing in the sight of the Lord; so He took his life also.

11    Then Judah said to his daughter-in-law Tamar, "Remain a widow in your father's house until my son Shelah grows up"; for he thought, *"I am afraid* that he too may die like his brothers." So Tamar went and lived in her father's house.

**12**    Now after a considerable time Shua's daughter, the wife of Judah, died; and when the time of mourning was ended, Judah went up to his sheepshearers at Timnah, he and his friend Hirah the Adullamite.

13    It was told to Tamar, "Behold, your father-in-law is going up to Timnah to shear his sheep."

14    So she removed her widow's garments and covered *herself* with a veil, and wrapped herself, and sat in the gateway of Enaim, which is on the road to Timnah; for she saw that Shelah had grown up, and she had not been given to him as a wife.

15    When Judah saw her, he thought she *was* a harlot, for she had covered her face.

16    So he turned aside to her by the road, and said, "Here now, let me come in to you"; for he did not know that she was his daughter-in-law. And she said, "What will you give me, that you may come in to me?"

17    He said, therefore, "I will send you a young goat from the flock." She said, moreover, "Will you give a pledge until you send *it*?"

18    He said, "What pledge shall I give you?" And she said, "Your seal and your cord, and your staff that is in your hand." So he gave *them* to her and went in to her, and she conceived by him.

19    Then she arose and departed, and removed her veil and put on her widow's garments.

**20**    When Judah sent the young goat by his friend the Adullamite, to receive the pledge from the woman's hand, he did not find her.

21    He asked the men of her place, saying, "Where is the temple prostitute who was by the road at Enaim?" But they said, "There has been no temple prostitute here."

22    So he returned to Judah, and said, "I did not find her; and furthermore, the men of the place said, 'There has been no temple prostitute here.'"

23    Then Judah said, "Let her keep them, otherwise we will become a laughingstock. After all, I sent this young goat, but you did not find her."

**24**    Now it was about three months later that Judah was informed, "Your daughter-in-law Tamar has played the harlot, and behold, she is also with child by harlotry." Then Judah said, "Bring her out and let her be burned!"

25    It was while she was being brought out that she sent to her father-in-law, saying, "I am with child by the man to whom these things belong." And she said, "Please examine and see, whose signet ring and cords and staff are these?"

26    Judah recognized *them*, and said, "She is more righteous than I, inasmuch as I did not give her to my son Shelah." And he did not have relations with her again.

**27**    It came about at the time she was giving birth, that behold, there were twins in her womb.

28    Moreover, it took place while she was giving birth, one put out a hand, and the midwife took and tied a scarlet *thread* on his hand, saying, "This one came out first."

29    But it came about as he drew back his hand, that behold, his brother came out. Then she said, "What a breach you have made for yourself!" So he was named Perez.

30    Afterward his brother came out who had the scarlet *thread* on his hand; and he was named Zerah.

## GENESIS 39
### Observation Worksheet

Chapter Theme _____

1    Now Joseph had been taken down to Egypt; and Potiphar, an Egyptian officer of Pharaoh, the captain of the bodyguard, bought him from the Ishmaelites, who had taken him down there.

2    The LORD was with Joseph, so he became a successful man. And he was in the house of his master, the Egyptian.

3    Now his master saw that the LORD was with him and *how* the LORD caused all that he did to prosper in his hand.

4    So Joseph found favor in his sight and became his personal servant; and he made him overseer over his house, and all that he owned he put in his charge.

5    It came about that from the time he made him overseer in his house and over all that he owned, the LORD blessed the Egyptian's house on account of Joseph; thus the LORD's blessing was upon all that he owned, in the house and in the field.

6    So he left everything he owned in Joseph's charge; and with him *there* he did not concern himself with anything except the food which he ate.
Now Joseph was handsome in form and appearance.

7    It came about after these events that his master's wife looked with desire at Joseph, and she said, "Lie with me."

8    But he refused and said to his master's wife, "Behold, with me *here*, my master does not concern himself with anything in the house, and he has put all that he owns in my charge.

9    "There is no one greater in this house than I, and he has withheld nothing from me except you, because you are his wife. How then could I do this great evil and sin against God?"

10  As she spoke to Joseph day after day, he did not listen to her to lie beside her *or* be with her.

11  Now it happened one day that he went into the house to do his work, and none of the men of the household was there inside.

12  She caught him by his garment, saying, "Lie with me!" And he left his garment in her hand and fled, and went outside.

13  When she saw that he had left his garment in her hand and had fled outside,

14  she called to the men of her household and said to them, "See, he has brought in a Hebrew to us to make sport of us; he came in to me to lie with me, and I screamed.

15  "When he heard that I raised my voice and screamed, he left his garment beside me and fled and went outside."

16  So she left his garment beside her until his master came home.

17  Then she spoke to him with these words, "The Hebrew slave, whom you brought to us, came in to me to make sport of me;

18  and as I raised my voice and screamed, he left his garment beside me and fled outside."

**19**  Now when his master heard the words of his wife, which she spoke to him, saying, "This is what your slave did to me," his anger burned.

20  So Joseph's master took him and put him into the jail, the place where the king's prisoners were confined; and he was there in the jail.

21  But the LORD was with Joseph and extended kindness to him, and gave him favor in the sight of the chief jailer.

22  The chief jailer committed to Joseph's charge all the prisoners who were in the jail; so that whatever was done there, he was responsible *for it*.

23  The chief jailer did not supervise anything under Joseph's charge because the LORD was with him; and whatever he did, the LORD made to prosper.

# GENESIS 40
## Observation Worksheet

Chapter Theme _____

1　Then it came about after these things, the cupbearer and the baker for the king of Egypt offended their lord, the king of Egypt.

2　Pharaoh was furious with his two officials, the chief cupbearer and the chief baker.

3　So he put them in confinement in the house of the captain of the bodyguard, in the jail, the *same* place where Joseph was imprisoned.

4　The captain of the bodyguard put Joseph in charge of them, and he took care of them; and they were in confinement for some time.

5　Then the cupbearer and the baker for the king of Egypt, who were confined in jail, both had a dream the same night, each man with his *own* dream *and* each dream with its *own* interpretation.

6　When Joseph came to them in the morning and observed them, behold, they were dejected.

7　He asked Pharaoh's officials who were with him in confinement in his master's house, "Why are your faces so sad today?"

8　Then they said to him, "We have had a dream and there is no one to interpret it." Then Joseph said to them, "Do not interpretations belong to God? Tell *it* to me, please."

9　So the chief cupbearer told his dream to Joseph, and said to him, "In my dream, behold, *there was* a vine in front of me;

10　and on the vine *were* three branches. And as it was budding, its blossoms came out, *and* its clusters produced ripe grapes.

11  "Now Pharaoh's cup was in my hand; so I took the grapes and squeezed them into Pharaoh's cup, and I put the cup into Pharaoh's hand."

12  Then Joseph said to him, "This is the interpretation of it: the three branches are three days;

13  within three more days Pharaoh will lift up your head and restore you to your office; and you will put Pharaoh's cup into his hand according to your former custom when you were his cupbearer.

14  "Only keep me in mind when it goes well with you, and please do me a kindness by mentioning me to Pharaoh and get me out of this house.

15  "For I was in fact kidnapped from the land of the Hebrews, and even here I have done nothing that they should have put me into the dungeon."

16  When the chief baker saw that he had interpreted favorably, he said to Joseph, "I also *saw* in my dream, and behold, *there were* three baskets of white bread on my head;

17  and in the top basket *there were* some of all sorts of baked food for Pharaoh, and the birds were eating them out of the basket on my head."

18  Then Joseph answered and said, "This is its interpretation: the three baskets are three days;

19  within three more days Pharaoh will lift up your head from you and will hang you on a tree, and the birds will eat your flesh off you."

20  Thus it came about on the third day, *which was* Pharaoh's birthday, that he made a feast for all his servants; and he lifted up the head of the chief cupbearer and the head of the chief baker among his servants.

21  He restored the chief cupbearer to his office, and he put the cup into Pharaoh's hand;

22  but he hanged the chief baker, just as Joseph had interpreted to them.

23  Yet the chief cupbearer did not remember Joseph, but forgot him.

# GENESIS 41
## Observation Worksheet

Chapter Theme _____

1  Now it happened at the end of two full years that Pharaoh had a dream, and behold, he was standing by the Nile.

2  And lo, from the Nile there came up seven cows, sleek and fat; and they grazed in the marsh grass.

3  Then behold, seven other cows came up after them from the Nile, ugly and gaunt, and they stood by the *other* cows on the bank of the Nile.

4  The ugly and gaunt cows ate up the seven sleek and fat cows. Then Pharaoh awoke.

5  He fell asleep and dreamed a second time; and behold, seven ears of grain came up on a single stalk, plump and good.

6  Then behold, seven ears, thin and scorched by the east wind, sprouted up after them.

7  The thin ears swallowed up the seven plump and full ears. Then Pharaoh awoke, and behold, *it was* a dream.

8  Now in the morning his spirit was troubled, so he sent and called for all the magicians of Egypt, and all its wise men. And Pharaoh told them his dreams, but there was no one who could interpret them to Pharaoh.

9  Then the chief cupbearer spoke to Pharaoh, saying, "I would make mention today of my *own* offenses.

10  "Pharaoh was furious with his servants, and he put me in confinement in the house of the captain of the bodyguard, *both* me and the chief baker.

11  "We had a dream on the same night, he and I; each of us dreamed according to the interpretation of his *own* dream.

12  "Now a Hebrew youth *was* with us there, a servant of the captain of the body-guard, and we related *them* to him, and he interpreted our dreams for us. To each one he interpreted according to his *own* dream.

13  "And just as he interpreted for us, so it happened; he restored me in my office, but he hanged him."

**14**  Then Pharaoh sent and called for Joseph, and they hurriedly brought him out of the dungeon; and when he had shaved himself and changed his clothes, he came to Pharaoh.

15  Pharaoh said to Joseph, "I have had a dream, but no one can interpret it; and I have heard it said about you, that when you hear a dream you can interpret it."

16  Joseph then answered Pharaoh, saying, "It is not in me; God will give Pharaoh a favorable answer."

17  So Pharaoh spoke to Joseph, "In my dream, behold, I was standing on the bank of the Nile;

18  and behold, seven cows, fat and sleek came up out of the Nile, and they grazed in the marsh grass.

19  "Lo, seven other cows came up after them, poor and very ugly and gaunt, such as I had never seen for ugliness in all the land of Egypt;

20  and the lean and ugly cows ate up the first seven fat cows.

21  "Yet when they had devoured them, it could not be detected that they had devoured them, for they were just as ugly as before. Then I awoke.

22  "I saw also in my dream, and behold, seven ears, full and good, came up on a single stalk;

23  and lo, seven ears, withered, thin, *and* scorched by the east wind, sprouted up after them;

24  and the thin ears swallowed the seven good ears. Then I told it to the magicians, but there was no one who could explain it to me."

**25**  Now Joseph said to Pharaoh, "Pharaoh's dreams are one *and the same;* God has told to Pharaoh what He is about to do.

26    "The seven good cows are seven years; and the seven good ears are seven years; the dreams are one *and the same*.

27    "The seven lean and ugly cows that came up after them are seven years, and the seven thin ears scorched by the east wind will be seven years of famine.

28    "It is as I have spoken to Pharaoh: God has shown to Pharaoh what He is about to do.

29    "Behold, seven years of great abundance are coming in all the land of Egypt;

30    and after them seven years of famine will come, and all the abundance will be forgotten in the land of Egypt, and the famine will ravage the land.

31    "So the abundance will be unknown in the land because of that subsequent famine; for it *will be* very severe.

32    "Now as for the repeating of the dream to Pharaoh twice, *it means* that the matter is determined by God, and God will quickly bring it about.

33    "Now let Pharaoh look for a man discerning and wise, and set him over the land of Egypt.

34    "Let Pharaoh take action to appoint overseers in charge of the land, and let him exact a fifth *of the produce* of the land of Egypt in the seven years of abundance.

35    "Then let them gather all the food of these good years that are coming, and store up the grain for food in the cities under Pharaoh's authority, and let them guard *it*.

36    "Let the food become as a reserve for the land for the seven years of famine which will occur in the land of Egypt, so that the land will not perish during the famine."

37    Now the proposal seemed good to Pharaoh and to all his servants.

38    Then Pharaoh said to his servants, "Can we find a man like this, in whom is a divine spirit?"

39    So Pharaoh said to Joseph, "Since God has informed you of all this, there is no one so discerning and wise as you are.

40  "You shall be over my house, and according to your command all my people shall do homage; only in the throne I will be greater than you."

41  Pharaoh said to Joseph, "See, I have set you over all the land of Egypt."

42  Then Pharaoh took off his signet ring from his hand and put it on Joseph's hand, and clothed him in garments of fine linen and put the gold necklace around his neck.

43  He had him ride in his second chariot; and they proclaimed before him, "Bow the knee!" And he set him over all the land of Egypt.

44  Moreover, Pharaoh said to Joseph, "*Though* I am Pharaoh, yet without your permission no one shall raise his hand or foot in all the land of Egypt."

45  Then Pharaoh named Joseph Zaphenath-paneah; and he gave him Asenath, the daughter of Potiphera priest of On, as his wife. And Joseph went forth over the land of Egypt.

**46**  Now Joseph was thirty years old when he stood before Pharaoh, king of Egypt. And Joseph went out from the presence of Pharaoh and went through all the land of Egypt.

47  During the seven years of plenty the land brought forth abundantly.

48  So he gathered all the food of *these* seven years which occurred in the land of Egypt and placed the food in the cities; he placed in every city the food from its own surrounding fields.

49  Thus Joseph stored up grain in great abundance like the sand of the sea, until he stopped measuring *it*, for it was beyond measure.

**50**  Now before the year of famine came, two sons were born to Joseph, whom Asenath, the daughter of Potiphera priest of On, bore to him.

51  Joseph named the firstborn Manasseh, "For," *he said,* "God has made me forget all my trouble and all my father's household."

52  He named the second Ephraim, "For," *he said,* "God has made me fruitful in the land of my affliction."

**53**  When the seven years of plenty which had been in the land of Egypt came to an end,

54    and the seven years of famine began to come, just as Joseph had said, then there was famine in all the lands, but in all the land of Egypt there was bread.

55    So when all the land of Egypt was famished, the people cried out to Pharaoh for bread; and Pharaoh said to all the Egyptians, "Go to Joseph; whatever he says to you, you shall do."

56    When the famine was *spread* over all the face of the earth, then Joseph opened all the storehouses, and sold to the Egyptians; and the famine was severe in the land of Egypt.

57    *The people of* all the earth came to Egypt to buy grain from Joseph, because the famine was severe in all the earth.

# GENESIS 42
## Observation Worksheet

Chapter Theme _____

1   Now Jacob saw that there was grain in Egypt, and Jacob said to his sons, "Why are you staring at one another?"

2   He said, "Behold, I have heard that there is grain in Egypt; go down there and buy *some* for us from that place, so that we may live and not die."

3   Then ten brothers of Joseph went down to buy grain from Egypt.

4   But Jacob did not send Joseph's brother Benjamin with his brothers, for he said, "I am afraid that harm may befall him."

5   So the sons of Israel came to buy grain among those who were coming, for the famine was in the land of Canaan *also*.

6   Now Joseph was the ruler over the land; he was the one who sold to all the people of the land. And Joseph's brothers came and bowed down to him with *their* faces to the ground.

7   When Joseph saw his brothers he recognized them, but he disguised himself to them and spoke to them harshly. And he said to them, "Where have you come from?" And they said, "From the land of Canaan, to buy food."

8   But Joseph had recognized his brothers, although they did not recognize him.

9   Joseph remembered the dreams which he had about them, and said to them, "You are spies; you have come to look at the undefended parts of our land."

10   Then they said to him, "No, my lord, but your servants have come to buy food."

11   "We are all sons of one man; we are honest men, your servants are not spies."

12    Yet he said to them, "No, but you have come to look at the undefended parts of our land!"

13    But they said, "Your servants are twelve brothers *in all,* the sons of one man in the land of Canaan; and behold, the youngest is with our father today, and one is no longer alive."

14    Joseph said to them, "It is as I said to you, you are spies;

15    by this you will be tested: by the life of Pharaoh, you shall not go from this place unless your youngest brother comes here!

16    "Send one of you that he may get your brother, while you remain confined, that your words may be tested, whether there is truth in you. But if not, by the life of Pharaoh, surely you are spies."

17    So he put them all together in prison for three days.

**18**    Now Joseph said to them on the third day, "Do this and live, for I fear God:

19    if you are honest men, let one of your brothers be confined in your prison; but as for *the rest of* you, go, carry grain for the famine of your households,

20    and bring your youngest brother to me, so your words may be verified, and you will not die." And they did so.

21    Then they said to one another, "Truly we are guilty concerning our brother, because we saw the distress of his soul when he pleaded with us, yet we would not listen; therefore this distress has come upon us."

22    Reuben answered them, saying, "Did I not tell you, 'Do not sin against the boy'; and you would not listen? Now comes the reckoning for his blood."

23    They did not know, however, that Joseph understood, for there was an interpreter between them.

24    He turned away from them and wept. But when he returned to them and spoke to them, he took Simeon from them and bound him before their eyes.

25    Then Joseph gave orders to fill their bags with grain and to restore every man's money in his sack, and to give them provisions for the journey. And thus it was done for them.

**26**    So they loaded their donkeys with their grain and departed from there.

27    As one *of them* opened his sack to give his donkey fodder at the lodging place, he saw his money; and behold, it was in the mouth of his sack.

28    Then he said to his brothers, "My money has been returned, and behold, it is even in my sack." And their hearts sank, and they *turned* trembling to one another, saying, "What is this that God has done to us?"

29    When they came to their father Jacob in the land of Canaan, they told him all that had happened to them, saying,

30    "The man, the lord of the land, spoke harshly with us, and took us for spies of the country.

31    "But we said to him, 'We are honest men; we are not spies.

32    'We are twelve brothers, sons of our father; one is no longer alive, and the youngest is with our father today in the land of Canaan.'

33    "The man, the lord of the land, said to us, 'By this I will know that you are honest men: leave one of your brothers with me and take *grain for* the famine of your households, and go.

34    'But bring your youngest brother to me that I may know that you are not spies, but honest men. I will give your brother to you, and you may trade in the land.' "

35    Now it came about as they were emptying their sacks, that behold, every man's bundle of money *was* in his sack; and when they and their father saw their bundles of money, they were dismayed.

36    Their father Jacob said to them, "You have bereaved me of my children: Joseph is no more, and Simeon is no more, and you would take Benjamin; all these things are against me."

37    Then Reuben spoke to his father, saying, "You may put my two sons to death if I do not bring him *back* to you; put him in my care, and I will return him to you."

38    But Jacob said, "My son shall not go down with you; for his brother is dead, and he alone is left. If harm should befall him on the journey you are taking, then you will bring my gray hair down to Sheol in sorrow."

# GENESIS 43
## Observation Worksheet

Chapter Theme _____

1    Now the famine was severe in the land.

2    So it came about when they had finished eating the grain which they had brought from Egypt, that their father said to them, "Go back, buy us a little food."

3    Judah spoke to him, however, saying, "The man solemnly warned us, 'You shall not see my face unless your brother is with you.'

4    "If you send our brother with us, we will go down and buy you food.

5    "But if you do not send *him*, we will not go down; for the man said to us, 'You will not see my face unless your brother is with you.' "

6    Then Israel said, "Why did you treat me so badly by telling the man whether you still had *another* brother?"

7    But they said, "The man questioned particularly about us and our relatives, saying, 'Is your father still alive? Have you *another* brother?' So we answered his questions. Could we possibly know that he would say, 'Bring your brother down'?"

8    Judah said to his father Israel, "Send the lad with me and we will arise and go, that we may live and not die, we as well as you and our little ones.

9    "I myself will be surety for him; you may hold me responsible for him. If I do not bring him *back* to you and set him before you, then let me bear the blame before you forever.

10   "For if we had not delayed, surely by now we could have returned twice."

11   Then their father Israel said to them, "If *it must be* so, then do this: take some of the best products of the land in your bags, and carry down to the man as a present, a little balm and a little honey, aromatic gum and myrrh, pistachio nuts and almonds.

12 "Take double *the* money in your hand, and take back in your hand the money that was returned in the mouth of your sacks; perhaps it was a mistake.

13 "Take your brother also, and arise, return to the man;

14 and may God Almighty grant you compassion in the sight of the man, so that he will release to you your other brother and Benjamin. And as for me, if I am bereaved of my children, I am bereaved."

15 So the men took this present, and they took double *the* money in their hand, and Benjamin; then they arose and went down to Egypt and stood before Joseph.

**16** When Joseph saw Benjamin with them, he said to his house steward, "Bring the men into the house, and slay an animal and make ready; for the men are to dine with me at noon."

17 So the man did as Joseph said, and brought the men to Joseph's house.

18 Now the men were afraid, because they were brought to Joseph's house; and they said, "*It is* because of the money that was returned in our sacks the first time that we are being brought in, that he may seek occasion against us and fall upon us, and take us for slaves with our donkeys."

19 So they came near to Joseph's house steward, and spoke to him at the entrance of the house,

20 and said, "Oh, my lord, we indeed came down the first time to buy food,

21 and it came about when we came to the lodging place, that we opened our sacks, and behold, each man's money was in the mouth of his sack, our money in full. So we have brought it back in our hand.

22 "We have also brought down other money in our hand to buy food; we do not know who put our money in our sacks."

23 He said, "Be at ease, do not be afraid. Your God and the God of your father has given you treasure in your sacks; I had your money." Then he brought Simeon out to them.

24 Then the man brought the men into Joseph's house and gave them water, and they washed their feet; and he gave their donkeys fodder.

25 So they prepared the present for Joseph's coming at noon; for they had heard that they were to eat a meal there.

**26** When Joseph came home, they brought into the house to him the present which was in their hand and bowed to the ground before him.

27 Then he asked them about their welfare, and said, "Is your old father well, of whom you spoke? Is he still alive?"

28 They said, "Your servant our father is well; he is still alive." They bowed down in homage.

29 As he lifted his eyes and saw his brother Benjamin, his mother's son, he said, "Is this your youngest brother, of whom you spoke to me?" And he said, "May God be gracious to you, my son."

30 Joseph hurried *out* for he was deeply stirred over his brother, and he sought *a place* to weep; and he entered his chamber and wept there.

31 Then he washed his face and came out; and he controlled himself and said, "Serve the meal."

32 So they served him by himself, and them by themselves, and the Egyptians who ate with him by themselves, because the Egyptians could not eat bread with the Hebrews, for that is loathsome to the Egyptians.

33 Now they were seated before him, the firstborn according to his birthright and the youngest according to his youth, and the men looked at one another in astonishment.

34 He took portions to them from his own table, but Benjamin's portion was five times as much as any of theirs. So they feasted and drank freely with him.

# GENESIS 44
## Observation Worksheet

Chapter Theme _____

1    Then he commanded his house steward, saying, "Fill the men's sacks with food, as much as they can carry, and put each man's money in the mouth of his sack.

2    "Put my cup, the silver cup, in the mouth of the sack of the youngest, and his money for the grain." And he did as Joseph had told *him*.

3    As soon as it was light, the men were sent away, they with their donkeys.

4    They had *just* gone out of the city, *and* were not far off, when Joseph said to his house steward, "Up, follow the men; and when you overtake them, say to them, 'Why have you repaid evil for good?

5    'Is not this the one from which my lord drinks and which he indeed uses for divination? You have done wrong in doing this.' "

6    So he overtook them and spoke these words to them.

7    They said to him, "Why does my lord speak such words as these? Far be it from your servants to do such a thing.

8    "Behold, the money which we found in the mouth of our sacks we have brought back to you from the land of Canaan. How then could we steal silver or gold from your lord's house?

9    "With whomever of your servants it is found, let him die, and we also will be my lord's slaves."

10   So he said, "Now let it also be according to your words; he with whom it is found shall be my slave, and *the rest of* you shall be innocent."

11   Then they hurried, each man lowered his sack to the ground, and each man opened his sack.

12   He searched, beginning with the oldest and ending with the youngest, and the cup was found in Benjamin's sack.

13    Then they tore their clothes, and when each man loaded his donkey, they returned to the city.

**14**    When Judah and his brothers came to Joseph's house, he was still there, and they fell to the ground before him.

15    Joseph said to them, "What is this deed that you have done? Do you not know that such a man as I can indeed practice divination?"

16    So Judah said, "What can we say to my lord? What can we speak? And how can we justify ourselves? God has found out the iniquity of your servants; behold, we are my lord's slaves, both we and the one in whose possession the cup has been found."

17    But he said, "Far be it from me to do this. The man in whose possession the cup has been found, he shall be my slave; but as for you, go up in peace to your father."

**18**    Then Judah approached him, and said, "Oh my lord, may your servant please speak a word in my lord's ears, and do not be angry with your servant; for you are equal to Pharaoh.

19    "My lord asked his servants, saying, 'Have you a father or a brother?'

20    "We said to my lord, 'We have an old father and a little child of *his* old age. Now his brother is dead, so he alone is left of his mother, and his father loves him.'

21    "Then you said to your servants, 'Bring him down to me that I may set my eyes on him.'

22    "But we said to my lord, 'The lad cannot leave his father, for if he should leave his father, his father would die.'

23    "You said to your servants, however, 'Unless your youngest brother comes down with you, you will not see my face again.'

24    "Thus it came about when we went up to your servant my father, we told him the words of my lord.

25    "Our father said, 'Go back, buy us a little food.'

26 "But we said, 'We cannot go down. If our youngest brother is with us, then we will go down; for we cannot see the man's face unless our youngest brother is with us.'

27 "Your servant my father said to us, 'You know that my wife bore me two sons;

28 and the one went out from me, and I said, "Surely he is torn in pieces," and I have not seen him since.

29 'If you take this one also from me, and harm befalls him, you will bring my gray hair down to Sheol in sorrow.'

30 "Now, therefore, when I come to your servant my father, and the lad is not with us, since his life is bound up in the lad's life,

31 when he sees that the lad is not *with us*, he will die. Thus your servants will bring the gray hair of your servant our father down to Sheol in sorrow.

32 "For your servant became surety for the lad to my father, saying, 'If I do not bring him *back* to you, then let me bear the blame before my father forever.'

33 "Now, therefore, please let your servant remain instead of the lad a slave to my lord, and let the lad go up with his brothers.

34 "For how shall I go up to my father if the lad is not with me—for fear that I see the evil that would overtake my father?"

# GENESIS 45
## Observation Worksheet

Chapter Theme _____

1  Then Joseph could not control himself before all those who stood by him, and he cried, "Have everyone go out from me." So there was no man with him when Joseph made himself known to his brothers.

2  He wept so loudly that the Egyptians heard *it*, and the household of Pharaoh heard *of it*.

3  Then Joseph said to his brothers, "I am Joseph! Is my father still alive?" But his brothers could not answer him, for they were dismayed at his presence.

4  Then Joseph said to his brothers, "Please come closer to me." And they came closer. And he said, "I am your brother Joseph, whom you sold into Egypt.

5  "Now do not be grieved or angry with yourselves, because you sold me here, for God sent me before you to preserve life.

6  "For the famine *has been* in the land these two years, and there are still five years in which there will be neither plowing nor harvesting.

7  "God sent me before you to preserve for you a remnant in the earth, and to keep you alive by a great deliverance.

8  "Now, therefore, it was not you who sent me here, but God; and He has made me a father to Pharaoh and lord of all his household and ruler over all the land of Egypt.

9  "Hurry and go up to my father, and say to him, 'Thus says your son Joseph, "God has made me lord of all Egypt; come down to me, do not delay.

10  "You shall live in the land of Goshen, and you shall be near me, you and your children and your children's children and your flocks and your herds and all that you have.

11  "There I will also provide for you, for there are still five years of famine *to come*, and you and your household and all that you have would be impoverished."  '

12 "Behold, your eyes see, and the eyes of my brother Benjamin *see*, that it is my mouth which is speaking to you.

13 "Now you must tell my father of all my splendor in Egypt, and all that you have seen; and you must hurry and bring my father down here."

14 Then he fell on his brother Benjamin's neck and wept, and Benjamin wept on his neck.

15 He kissed all his brothers and wept on them, and afterward his brothers talked with him.

16 Now when the news was heard in Pharaoh's house that Joseph's brothers had come, it pleased Pharaoh and his servants.

17 Then Pharaoh said to Joseph, "Say to your brothers, 'Do this: load your beasts and go to the land of Canaan,

18 and take your father and your households and come to me, and I will give you the best of the land of Egypt and you will eat the fat of the land.'

19 "Now you are ordered, 'Do this: take wagons from the land of Egypt for your little ones and for your wives, and bring your father and come.

20 'Do not concern yourselves with your goods, for the best of all the land of Egypt is yours.' "

21 Then the sons of Israel did so; and Joseph gave them wagons according to the command of Pharaoh, and gave them provisions for the journey.

22 To each of them he gave changes of garments, but to Benjamin he gave three hundred *pieces of* silver and five changes of garments.

23 To his father he sent as follows: ten donkeys loaded with the best things of Egypt, and ten female donkeys loaded with grain and bread and sustenance for his father on the journey.

24 So he sent his brothers away, and as they departed, he said to them, "Do not quarrel on the journey."

25 Then they went up from Egypt, and came to the land of Canaan to their father Jacob.

26   They told him, saying, "Joseph is still alive, and indeed he is ruler over all the land of Egypt." But he was stunned, for he did not believe them.

27   When they told him all the words of Joseph that he had spoken to them, and when he saw the wagons that Joseph had sent to carry him, the spirit of their father Jacob revived.

28   Then Israel said, "It is enough; my son Joseph is still alive. I will go and see him before I die."

# GENESIS 46
## Observation Worksheet

Chapter Theme _____

1   So Israel set out with all that he had, and came to Beersheba, and offered sacrifices to the God of his father Isaac.

2   God spoke to Israel in visions of the night and said, "Jacob, Jacob." And he said, "Here I am."

3   He said, "I am God, the God of your father; do not be afraid to go down to Egypt, for I will make you a great nation there.

4   "I will go down with you to Egypt, and I will also surely bring you up again; and Joseph will close your eyes."

5   Then Jacob arose from Beersheba; and the sons of Israel carried their father Jacob and their little ones and their wives in the wagons which Pharaoh had sent to carry him.

6   They took their livestock and their property, which they had acquired in the land of Canaan, and came to Egypt, Jacob and all his descendants with him:

7   his sons and his grandsons with him, his daughters and his granddaughters, and all his descendants he brought with him to Egypt.

8   Now these are the names of the sons of Israel, Jacob and his sons, who went to Egypt: Reuben, Jacob's firstborn.

9   The sons of Reuben: Hanoch and Pallu and Hezron and Carmi.

10  The sons of Simeon: Jemuel and Jamin and Ohad and Jachin and Zohar and Shaul the son of a Canaanite woman.

11  The sons of Levi: Gershon, Kohath, and Merari.

12  The sons of Judah: Er and Onan and Shelah and Perez and Zerah (but Er and Onan died in the land of Canaan). And the sons of Perez were Hezron and Hamul.

13  The sons of Issachar: Tola and Puvvah and Iob and Shimron.

14    The sons of Zebulun: Sered and Elon and Jahleel.

15    These are the sons of Leah, whom she bore to Jacob in Paddan-aram, with his daughter Dinah; all his sons and his daughters *numbered* thirty-three.

16    The sons of Gad: Ziphion and Haggi, Shuni and Ezbon, Eri and Arodi and Areli.

17    The sons of Asher: Imnah and Ishvah and Ishvi and Beriah and their sister Serah. And the sons of Beriah: Heber and Malchiel.

18    These are the sons of Zilpah, whom Laban gave to his daughter Leah; and she bore to Jacob these sixteen persons.

19    The sons of Jacob's wife Rachel: Joseph and Benjamin.

20    Now to Joseph in the land of Egypt were born Manasseh and Ephraim, whom Asenath, the daughter of Potiphera, priest of On, bore to him.

21    The sons of Benjamin: Bela and Becher and Ashbel, Gera and Naaman, Ehi and Rosh, Muppim and Huppim and Ard.

22    These are the sons of Rachel, who were born to Jacob; *there were* fourteen persons in all.

23    The sons of Dan: Hushim.

24    The sons of Naphtali: Jahzeel and Guni and Jezer and Shillem.

25    These are the sons of Bilhah, whom Laban gave to his daughter Rachel, and she bore these to Jacob; *there were* seven persons in all.

26    All the persons belonging to Jacob, who came to Egypt, his direct descendants, not including the wives of Jacob's sons, *were* sixty-six persons in all,

27    and the sons of Joseph, who were born to him in Egypt were two; all the persons of the house of Jacob, who came to Egypt, *were* seventy.

**28**    Now he sent Judah before him to Joseph, to point out *the way* before him to Goshen; and they came into the land of Goshen.

29    Joseph prepared his chariot and went up to Goshen to meet his father Israel; as soon as he appeared before him, he fell on his neck and wept on his neck a long time.

30    Then Israel said to Joseph, "Now let me die, since I have seen your face, that you are still alive."

31    Joseph said to his brothers and to his father's household, "I will go up and tell Pharaoh, and will say to him, 'My brothers and my father's household, who *were* in the land of Canaan, have come to me;

32    and the men are shepherds, for they have been keepers of livestock; and they have brought their flocks and their herds and all that they have.'

33    "When Pharaoh calls you and says, 'What is your occupation?'

34    you shall say, 'Your servants have been keepers of livestock from our youth even until now, both we and our fathers,' that you may live in the land of Goshen; for every shepherd is loathsome to the Egyptians."

## GENESIS 47
### Observation Worksheet

Chapter Theme _____

1   Then Joseph went in and told Pharaoh, and said, "My father and my brothers and their flocks and their herds and all that they have, have come out of the land of Canaan; and behold, they are in the land of Goshen."

2   He took five men from among his brothers and presented them to Pharaoh.

3   Then Pharaoh said to his brothers, "What is your occupation?" So they said to Pharaoh, "Your servants are shepherds, both we and our fathers."

4   They said to Pharaoh, "We have come to sojourn in the land, for there is no pasture for your servants' flocks, for the famine is severe in the land of Canaan. Now, therefore, please let your servants live in the land of Goshen."

5   Then Pharaoh said to Joseph, "Your father and your brothers have come to you.

6   "The land of Egypt is at your disposal; settle your father and your brothers in the best of the land, let them live in the land of Goshen; and if you know any capable men among them, then put them in charge of my livestock."

7   Then Joseph brought his father Jacob and presented him to Pharaoh; and Jacob blessed Pharaoh.

8   Pharaoh said to Jacob, "How many years have you lived?"

9   So Jacob said to Pharaoh, "The years of my sojourning are one hundred and thirty; few and unpleasant have been the years of my life, nor have they attained the years that my fathers lived during the days of their sojourning."

10  And Jacob blessed Pharaoh, and went out from his presence.

11  So Joseph settled his father and his brothers and gave them a possession in the land of Egypt, in the best of the land, in the land of Rameses, as Pharaoh had ordered.

12  Joseph provided his father and his brothers and all his father's household with food, according to their little ones.

13   Now there was no food in all the land, because the famine was very severe, so that the land of Egypt and the land of Canaan languished because of the famine.

14   Joseph gathered all the money that was found in the land of Egypt and in the land of Canaan for the grain which they bought, and Joseph brought the money into Pharaoh's house.

15   When the money was all spent in the land of Egypt and in the land of Canaan, all the Egyptians came to Joseph and said, "Give us food, for why should we die in your presence? For *our* money is gone."

16   Then Joseph said, "Give up your livestock, and I will give you *food* for your livestock, since *your* money is gone."

17   So they brought their livestock to Joseph, and Joseph gave them food in exchange for the horses and the flocks and the herds and the donkeys; and he fed them with food in exchange for all their livestock that year.

18   When that year was ended, they came to him the next year and said to him, "We will not hide from my lord that our money is all spent, and the cattle are my lord's. There is nothing left for my lord except our bodies and our lands.

19   "Why should we die before your eyes, both we and our land? Buy us and our land for food, and we and our land will be slaves to Pharaoh. So give us seed, that we may live and not die, and that the land may not be desolate."

20   So Joseph bought all the land of Egypt for Pharaoh, for every Egyptian sold his field, because the famine was severe upon them. Thus the land became Pharaoh's.

21   As for the people, he removed them to the cities from one end of Egypt's border to the other.

22   Only the land of the priests he did not buy, for the priests had an allotment from Pharaoh, and they lived off the allotment which Pharaoh gave them. Therefore, they did not sell their land.

23   Then Joseph said to the people, "Behold, I have today bought you and your land for Pharaoh; now, *here* is seed for you, and you may sow the land.

24   "At the harvest you shall give a fifth to Pharaoh, and four-fifths shall be your own for seed of the field and for your food and for those of your households and as food for your little ones."

25   So they said, "You have saved our lives! Let us find favor in the sight of my lord, and we will be Pharaoh's slaves."

26   Joseph made it a statute concerning the land of Egypt *valid* to this day, that Pharaoh should have the fifth; only the land of the priests did not become Pharaoh's.

**27**   Now Israel lived in the land of Egypt, in Goshen, and they acquired property in it and were fruitful and became very numerous.

28   Jacob lived in the land of Egypt seventeen years; so the length of Jacob's life was one hundred and forty-seven years.

**29**   When the time for Israel to die drew near, he called his son Joseph and said to him, "Please, if I have found favor in your sight, place now your hand under my thigh and deal with me in kindness and faithfulness. Please do not bury me in Egypt,

30   but when I lie down with my fathers, you shall carry me out of Egypt and bury me in their burial place." And he said, "I will do as you have said."

31   He said, "Swear to me." So he swore to him. Then Israel bowed *in worship* at the head of the bed.

# GENESIS 48
## Observation Worksheet

Chapter Theme _____

1   Now it came about after these things that Joseph was told, "Behold, your father is sick." So he took his two sons Manasseh and Ephraim with him.

2   When it was told to Jacob, "Behold, your son Joseph has come to you," Israel collected his strength and sat up in the bed.

3   Then Jacob said to Joseph, "God Almighty appeared to me at Luz in the land of Canaan and blessed me,

4   and He said to me, 'Behold, I will make you fruitful and numerous, and I will make you a company of peoples, and will give this land to your descendants after you for an everlasting possession.'

5   "Now your two sons, who were born to you in the land of Egypt before I came to you in Egypt, are mine; Ephraim and Manasseh shall be mine, as Reuben and Simeon are.

6   "But your offspring that have been born after them shall be yours; they shall be called by the names of their brothers in their inheritance.

7   "Now as for me, when I came from Paddan, Rachel died, to my sorrow, in the land of Canaan on the journey, when there was still some distance to go to Ephrath; and I buried her there on the way to Ephrath (that is, Bethlehem)."

8   When Israel saw Joseph's sons, he said, "Who are these?"

9   Joseph said to his father, "They are my sons, whom God has given me here." So he said, "Bring them to me, please, that I may bless them."

10  Now the eyes of Israel were *so* dim from age *that* he could not see. Then Joseph brought them close to him, and he kissed them and embraced them.

11  Israel said to Joseph, "I never expected to see your face, and behold, God has let me see your children as well."

12  Then Joseph took them from his knees, and bowed with his face to the ground.

13     Joseph took them both, Ephraim with his right hand toward Israel's left, and Manasseh with his left hand toward Israel's right, and brought them close to him.

14     But Israel stretched out his right hand and laid it on the head of Ephraim, who was the younger, and his left hand on Manasseh's head, crossing his hands, although Manasseh was the firstborn.

15     He blessed Joseph, and said,

> "The God before whom my fathers Abraham and Isaac walked,
>
> The God who has been my shepherd all my life to this day,

16         The angel who has redeemed me from all evil,

> Bless the lads;
>
> And may my name live on in them,
>
> And the names of my fathers Abraham and Isaac;
>
> And may they grow into a multitude in the midst of the earth."

17     When Joseph saw that his father laid his right hand on Ephraim's head, it displeased him; and he grasped his father's hand to remove it from Ephraim's head to Manasseh's head.

18     Joseph said to his father, "Not so, my father, for this one is the firstborn. Place your right hand on his head."

19     But his father refused and said, "I know, my son, I know; he also will become a people and he also will be great. However, his younger brother shall be greater than he, and his descendants shall become a multitude of nations."

20     He blessed them that day, saying,

> "By you Israel will pronounce blessing, saying,
>
> 'May God make you like Ephraim and Manasseh!' "

Thus he put Ephraim before Manasseh.

21     Then Israel said to Joseph, "Behold, I am about to die, but God will be with you, and bring you back to the land of your fathers.

22     "I give you one portion more than your brothers, which I took from the hand of the Amorite with my sword and my bow."

# GENESIS 49
## Observation Worksheet

Chapter Theme _____

1  Then Jacob summoned his sons and said, "Assemble yourselves that I may tell you
   what will befall you in the days to come.

2  "Gather together and hear, O sons of Jacob;
   And listen to Israel your father.

**3**  "Reuben, you are my firstborn;
   My might and the beginning of my strength,
   Preeminent in dignity and preeminent in power.

4  "Uncontrolled as water, you shall not have preeminence,
   Because you went up to your father's bed;
   Then you defiled *it*—he went up to my couch.

**5**  "Simeon and Levi are brothers;
   Their swords are implements of violence.

6  "Let my soul not enter into their council;
   Let not my glory be united with their assembly;
   Because in their anger they slew men,
   And in their self-will they lamed oxen.

7  "Cursed be their anger, for it is fierce;
   And their wrath, for it is cruel.
   I will disperse them in Jacob,
   And scatter them in Israel.

**8**  "Judah, your brothers shall praise you;
   Your hand shall be on the neck of your enemies;
   Your father's sons shall bow down to you.

9 "Judah is a lion's whelp;

  From the prey, my son, you have gone up.

  He couches, he lies down as a lion,

  And as a lion, who dares rouse him up?

10 "The scepter shall not depart from Judah,

  Nor the ruler's staff from between his feet,

  Until Shiloh comes,

  And to him *shall be* the obedience of the peoples.

11 "He ties *his* foal to the vine,

  And his donkey's colt to the choice vine;

  He washes his garments in wine,

  And his robes in the blood of grapes.

12 "His eyes are dull from wine,

  And his teeth white from milk.

**13** "Zebulun will dwell at the seashore;

  And he *shall be* a haven for ships,

  And his flank *shall be* toward Sidon.

**14** "Issachar is a strong donkey,

  Lying down between the sheepfolds.

15 "When he saw that a resting place was good

  And that the land was pleasant,

  He bowed his shoulder to bear *burdens*,

  And became a slave at forced labor.

**16** "Dan shall judge his people,

  As one of the tribes of Israel.

17 "Dan shall be a serpent in the way,

  A horned snake in the path,

  That bites the horse's heels,

  So that his rider falls backward.

18    "For Your salvation I wait, O L<small>ORD</small>.

**19**    "As for Gad, raiders shall raid him,

        But he will raid *at* their heels.

**20**    "As for Asher, his food shall be rich,

        And he will yield royal dainties.

**21**    "Naphtali is a doe let loose,

        He gives beautiful words.

**22**    "Joseph is a fruitful bough,

        A fruitful bough by a spring;

        *Its* branches run over a wall.

23    "The archers bitterly attacked him,

        And shot *at him* and harassed him;

24    But his bow remained firm,

        And his arms were agile,

        From the hands of the Mighty One of Jacob

        (From there is the Shepherd, the Stone of Israel),

25    From the God of your father who helps you,

        And by the Almighty who blesses you

        *With* blessings of heaven above,

        Blessings of the deep that lies beneath,

        Blessings of the breasts and of the womb.

26    "The blessings of your father

        Have surpassed the blessings of my ancestors

        Up to the utmost bound of the everlasting hills;

        May they be on the head of Joseph,

        And on the crown of the head of the one distinguished among his brothers.

27    "Benjamin is a ravenous wolf;

        In the morning he devours the prey,

        And in the evening he divides the spoil."

**28**   All these are the twelve tribes of Israel, and this is what their father said to them when he blessed them. He blessed them, every one with the blessing appropriate to him.

**29**   Then he charged them and said to them, "I am about to be gathered to my people; bury me with my fathers in the cave that is in the field of Ephron the Hittite,

**30**   in the cave that is in the field of Machpelah, which is before Mamre, in the land of Canaan, which Abraham bought along with the field from Ephron the Hittite for a burial site.

**31**   "There they buried Abraham and his wife Sarah, there they buried Isaac and his wife Rebekah, and there I buried Leah—

**32**   the field and the cave that is in it, purchased from the sons of Heth."

**33**   When Jacob finished charging his sons, he drew his feet into the bed and breathed his last, and was gathered to his people.

# GENESIS 50
## Observation Worksheet

Chapter Theme _____

1   Then Joseph fell on his father's face, and wept over him and kissed him.

2   Joseph commanded his servants the physicians to embalm his father. So the physicians embalmed Israel.

3   Now forty days were required for it, for such is the period required for embalming. And the Egyptians wept for him seventy days.

4   When the days of mourning for him were past, Joseph spoke to the household of Pharaoh, saying, "If now I have found favor in your sight, please speak to Pharaoh, saying,

5   'My father made me swear, saying, "Behold, I am about to die; in my grave which I dug for myself in the land of Canaan, there you shall bury me." Now therefore, please let me go up and bury my father; then I will return.' "

6   Pharaoh said, "Go up and bury your father, as he made you swear."

7   So Joseph went up to bury his father, and with him went up all the servants of Pharaoh, the elders of his household and all the elders of the land of Egypt,

8   and all the household of Joseph and his brothers and his father's household; they left only their little ones and their flocks and their herds in the land of Goshen.

9   There also went up with him both chariots and horsemen; and it was a very great company.

10   When they came to the threshing floor of Atad, which is beyond the Jordan, they lamented there with a very great and sorrowful lamentation; and he observed seven days mourning for his father.

11   Now when the inhabitants of the land, the Canaanites, saw the mourning at the threshing floor of Atad, they said, "This is a grievous mourning for the Egyptians." Therefore it was named Abel-mizraim, which is beyond the Jordan.

12   Thus his sons did for him as he had charged them;

13     for his sons carried him to the land of Canaan and buried him in the cave of the field of Machpelah before Mamre, which Abraham had bought along with the field for a burial site from Ephron the Hittite.

14     After he had buried his father, Joseph returned to Egypt, he and his brothers, and all who had gone up with him to bury his father.

**15**     When Joseph's brothers saw that their father was dead, they said, "What if Joseph bears a grudge against us and pays us back in full for all the wrong which we did to him!"

16     So they sent *a message* to Joseph, saying, "Your father charged before he died, saying,

17     'Thus you shall say to Joseph, "Please forgive, I beg you, the transgression of your brothers and their sin, for they did you wrong." ' And now, please forgive the transgression of the servants of the God of your father." And Joseph wept when they spoke to him.

18     Then his brothers also came and fell down before him and said, "Behold, we are your servants."

19     But Joseph said to them, "Do not be afraid, for am I in God's place?

20     "As for you, you meant evil against me, *but* God meant it for good in order to bring about this present result, to preserve many people alive.

21     "So therefore, do not be afraid; I will provide for you and your little ones." So he comforted them and spoke kindly to them.

**22**     Now Joseph stayed in Egypt, he and his father's household, and Joseph lived one hundred and ten years.

23     Joseph saw the third generation of Ephraim's sons; also the sons of Machir, the son of Manasseh, were born on Joseph's knees.

24     Joseph said to his brothers, "I am about to die, but God will surely take care of you and bring you up from this land to the land which He promised on oath to Abraham, to Isaac and to Jacob."

25     Then Joseph made the sons of Israel swear, saying, "God will surely take care of you, and you shall carry my bones up from here."

26    So Joseph died at the age of one hundred and ten years; and he was embalmed and placed in a coffin in Egypt.

# AT A GLANCE CHART

BOOK THEME:

KEY
WORDS &
PHRASES:

CHAPTER
THEMES:

| | |
|---|---|
| 1 | Creation in Six Days |
| 2 | Creation of Mankind |
| 3 | The Fall |
| 4 | Cain and Abel |
| 5 | Life under the Curse |
| 6 | Setting for the Flood Judgment |
| 7 | The Flood |
| 8 | The End of the Flood |
| 9 | God's Covenant with Noah |
| 10 | Nations Separated after the Flood |
| 11 | Babel |
| 12 | God Calls Abram/Abram & Pharaoh |
| 13 | Abram and Lot Separate |
| 14 | Abram rescues Lot/Melchizedek |
| 15 | God's covenant with Abram |
| 16 | Hagar bears Ishmael |
| 17 | Circumcision – Sign of the Covenant |
| 18 | Promise of Isaac/Abraham intercedes for Sodom |
| 19 | Destruction of Sodom & Gomorrah |
| 20 | Abraham & Abimelech |
| 21 | Sarah bears Isaac |
| 22 | Abraham offers Isaac |
| 23 | Sarah buried at Hebron |
| 24 | Rebekah becomes Isaac's Wife |
| 25 | Abraham marries Keturah/Dies/Jacob & Esau |

# AT A GLANCE CHART

KEY
WORDS &
PHRASES:

CHAPTER
THEMES:

| | |
|---|---|
| 26 | God's Covenant with Isaac/Isaac & Abimelech |
| 27 | Isaac Blesses Jacob |
| 28 | God's Promise to Jacob/Jacob's Vow to God |
| 29 | Jacob serves for Leah and Rachel |
| 30 | Jacob's Children/Prospers |
| 31 | Jacob's Covenant with Laban |
| 32 | Gifts for Esau/Jacob Wrestles |
| 33 | Jacob Meets Esau/Settles in Shechem |
| 34 | Dinah & Sheckem |
| 35 | Jacob to Bethel/Benjamin born/Rachel dies |
| 36 | Generations of Esau |
| 37 | |
| 38 | |
| 39 | |
| 40 | |
| 41 | |
| 42 | |
| 43 | |
| 44 | |
| 45 | |
| 46 | |
| 47 | |
| 48 | |
| 49 | |
| 50 | |

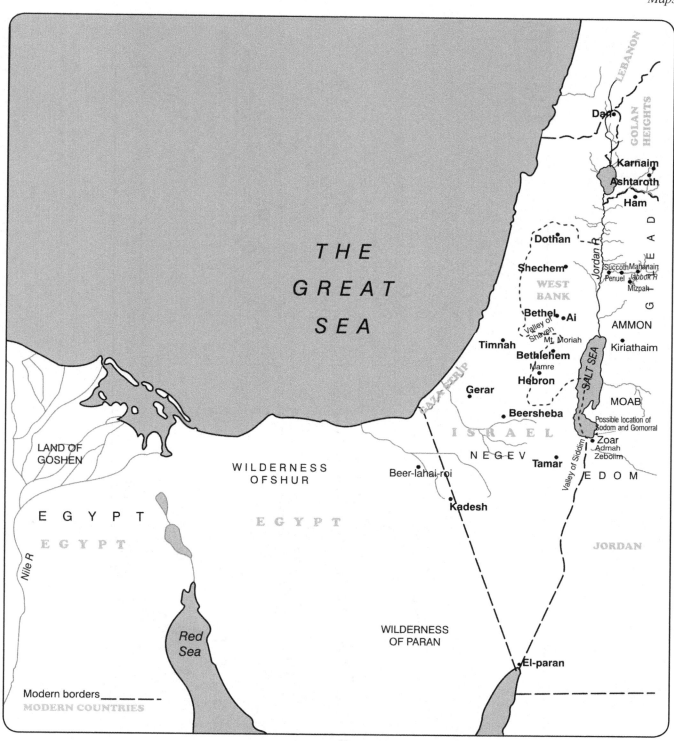

THE
GREAT
SEA

LEBANON

GOLAN
HEIGHTS

Dan

Karnaim
Ashtaroth
Ham

G I L E A D

Dothan
Shechem
Succoth Mahanaim
Penuel Jabbok R
Mizpah

WEST
BANK

Bethel • Ai
Valley of
Shaveh
Mt. Moriah

Timnah
Bethlehem
Mamre
Hebron

Jordan R

AMMON

Kiriathaim

SALT SEA

MOAB

Gerar
Beersheba

Possible location of
Sodom and Gomorral

GAZA STRIP

I S R A E L

Zoar
Admah
Zeboiim

N E G E V

Tamar

Valley of Siddim

E D O M

Beer-lahai-roi

Kadesh

LAND OF
GOSHEN

WILDERNESS
OF SHUR

E G Y P T

E G Y P T
E G Y P T

Nile R

Red
Sea

WILDERNESS
OF PARAN

JORDAN

El-paran

Modern borders _ _ _ _ _
MODERN COUNTRIES

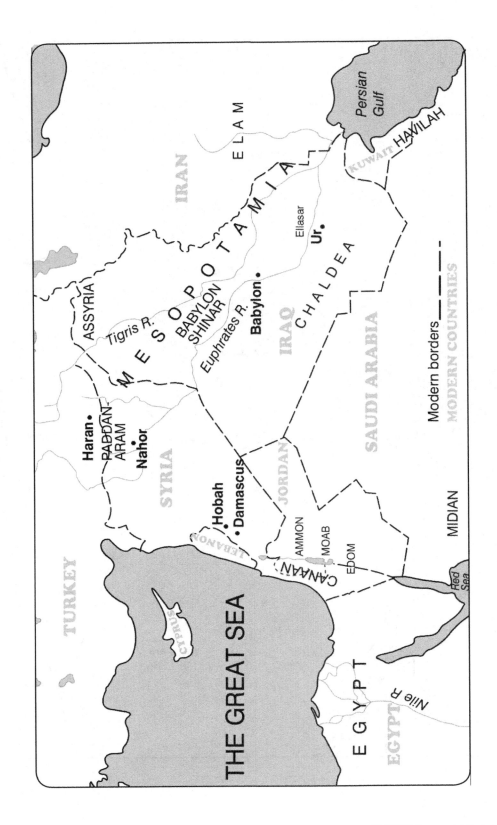

*Joseph*

*Joseph*

CPSIA information can be obtained at www.ICGtesting.com
Printed in the USA
LVOW03s2317130915
453965LV00009B/24/P